DESIGNING WITH

FABRIC

The Creative Touch

Carol Soucek King, Ph.D.

Foreword by Stanley Abercrombie, FAIA

Interior Details

AN IMPRINT OF
PBC INTERNATIONAL, INC.

Distributor to the book trade in the United States and Canada
Rizzoli International Publications
through St. Martin's Press
175 Fifth Avenue
New York, NY 10010

Distributor to the art trade in the United States and Canada
PBC International, Inc.
One School Street
Glen Cove, NY 11542

Distributor throughout the rest of the world
Hearst Books International
1350 Avenue of the Americas
New York, NY 10019

Library of Congress Cataloging–in–Publication Data

King, Carol Soucek.
Designing with fabric: the creative touch / by Carol Soucek King.
      p.   cm.
   Includes index.
   ISBN 0-86636-331-9 (hardcover : alk. paper). -- ISBN 0-86636-485-4 (paperbound)
   (pbk. : alk. paper)
   1. Textile fabrics in interior decoration I. Title
NK2115.5.F3K56 1996   96–45172
747'.9—dc20   CIP

CAVEAT– Information in this text is believed accurate, and will pose no
problem for the student or casual reader. However, the author was often
constrained by information contained in signed release forms, information
that could have been in error or not included at all. Any misinformation
(or lack of information) is the result of failure in these attestations. The
author has done whatever is possible to insure accuracy.

Designed by Garrett Schuh

Color separation by
Fine Arts Repro House Co., Ltd., H.K.
Printed in Hong Kong by South China Printing Co. (1988) Ltd.

10 9 8 7 6 5 4 3 2 1

Printed in Hong Kong

To Creativity at Home...
and Being at Home with Creativity!

Contents

FOREWORD

Sorry to repeat myself, but in the last sentence of a book titled
A Philosophy of Interior Design, I wrote that interiors constitute "our
most personal art." Carol Soucek King, I'm glad to see, seems to share
the same view, for the admirable series of books Dr. King has planned
promises to focus on just those aspects of interior design that make
it personal.

The grand concept is not to be neglected, of course. Like any other art,
interior design depends for its success on the encompassing vision that
relates its many elements in a meaningful whole. But such vision, in
interiors, becomes manifest and comprehensible through the medium of
myriad details with which we are in intimate contact: the feel of a drawer-
pull, the profile of a cornice, the polish and grain of wood, the "hand"
of fabric.

This contact involves all our senses. We see our interiors, certainly, but
we also smell the materials in them, we hear their acoustic properties, we
brush up against their walls, step on their floors, open their casegoods, sit
on their chairs. More than any other, interior design is the art we use.
In that sense, it is not only our most personal art, but also the one most
responsible for our well-being. In the context of increasingly brutalized
urban environments, this is increasingly true and increasingly important.
Interior design is often our refuge.

It is therefore a very welcome prospect that Dr. King is turning her expe-
rienced editorial eye to the details and materials on which the art of interior design depends. I'm sure we will all benefit from her discoveries.

Stanley Abercrombie, FAIA
Chief Editor, INTERIOR DESIGN

PREFACE

To some, a book devoted to the idea of fabrics as integral to structure may come as a surprise. Yet the fact is that fabrics used to dress walls, floors, windows, ceilings and dividers in between define space the same way that heftier building materials do but with a visual, tactile poetry all their own.

Seen as an exciting, pliable complement to less malleable surfaces such as tile, stone, brick, wood and glass, fabric provides a feeling of warmth and offers an endless variety of texture, pattern, color and even reflectivity. And today, the combination of age-old crafts, refined skills and modern technologies makes fabrics more functional than ever before and possibly even more glorious.

From the sensuously padded upholstered wall to a tautly woven metal one, from ceiling treatments gathered and draped to ones precisely backed for flat application, fabrics offer enrichment and individuality amid our too-often impersonal and hard-edged world. In the following homes from around the world, leading architects and designers share their reasons for selecting either glimmering silk or handwoven cotton, either prints or solids, either sculptured or flat applications. They show how fabrics can be used to embellish large spaces or, conversely, to simplify and thereby visually enlarge small ones. They reveal what works best in climates both humid and dry, and how pattern and color can be used in ways both traditional and innovative.

Exploring the varieties of fabric and gaining an insight into the infinite ways it can be used is an essential ingredient in understanding how to bring character and beauty to our homes. For those who seek good design as an element by which they can empower their lives, I hope this book will contribute to their quest.

Carol Soucek King, Ph.D.

INTRODUCTION

This last volume in Dr. King's all-encompassing series of four books embracing
the wide-ranging subject of materials for the home addresses one of the
oldest artistic expressions of man's creative use of his surroundings. The
textile industry is today the seventh-largest industry on the planet. Contem-
plate the range and history of textile use and you understand the depth of Dr.
King's subject.

The production of textiles is one of civilization's earliest accomplishments. It
reflects man's successful struggle to control and adapt himself to his environment. The history of textiles is 8,000 years old, and developments have been
constant and phenomenal. Textiles, useful and practical as they are, have always
played a role in the history and technical and stylistic evolution of art.

The famous traveler and giant of commerce, Marco Polo, spent his life in search
of spices and textiles — so basic and luxurious were they considered. Humans
have ceaselessly collected rare and innovative cloth. Today, museums are full of
those masterpieces and it is taken for granted that everyone interested in interior
design is interested in fabric and attracted to how it feels, catches the light, folds
and responds to draping or stitching, and its various uses. It is vitally important
that anyone in interior design today be educated and well read in the field of
textiles especially. So many technical problems can occur in both weaving and
printing, and techniques are very complicated, the terminology is unfamiliar
and sometimes outdated. So much is still done by hand, like dying and silk
screen printing, but, at the same time, those ancient arts are being harnessed
into stability by using computers and swiftly advancing new machinery.

Textiles play a vital part in daily life as clothing, bedding, rugs, linens, upholstery, lamp shades, slipcovers, draperies, trims and ribbons, curtains and shades.
They are also vital in industry — automotive, aviation, fishing, sailing, military
and space. Yet most people actually know very little of the part they play. It is
as if this knowledge were beyond their reach. This is why books like Dr. King's
are so very important.

People express their creativity, style, culture and achievements through their
homes, and textiles are foremost in those expressions. Exquisitely executed and
masterfully designed cloth will always distinguish rooms that are tasteful as well
as fashionable from those that are ordinary. Subtlety is masterful, and subtly

ABOVE *A restrained dark
blue-and-white toile and
wide blue-and-white stripe,
combined with two antique
quilts, create a dramatic bedroom setting in Suzanne
Varney's home. Both fabrics
are from Carleton V Ltd.*

*Photography courtesy of
Carleton V Ltd.*

created pattern using splendid yarn makes a room elegant, sensuous and easier to live in ... but at the same time, craft and ethnic textiles have the ability to create drama as well as solid comfort. There are cloths for everyone, every time, everywhere, and fabric itself has sparked a wealth of various artistic expressions having pattern, yarn and color as their inspiration.

Textiles transport easily and express cultural history. In ancient times the people of China, India, Egypt, Persia and Turkistan were using padded fabric for bedding, clothing and even armor. The Romans, those sophisticates, had quilted mattresses, bedcovers and cushions. Somewhere between the thirteenth and fifteenth centuries, the Crusaders found quilted garments on the bodies of their enemies, the Saracens. The art of quilting for beauty as well as utility grew up and, I believe, achieved its highest, brightest moment here in America. Quilts from the various American museums could tell the story of the United States from the earliest days.

Many authors have tried to convey the complexity of the subject of textiles and their uses, and Dr. King's exploration seeks to broaden her readers' viewpoint and make reading about life with textiles a twenty-first-century adventure. She relays her excitement about cloth, its magical qualities, its magnificent range and its workhorse strength and brings her reader closer to textiles.

Love of textiles is universal; it cuts through cultural differences and global distances. The weaver in the smallest village in Ecuador has much in common with the silk weaver of Lyon or the tapa maker in Polynesia or Africa. Their work produces the story of mankind as it comes from the soul of creativity and invents its own technology. The challenge is to use technology to man's advantage without losing the elusive quality found in textiles ... deepest human expression.

Suzanne Varney
President, CARLETON V LTD.
President, DECORATIVE FABRICS ASSOCIATION

Multicultural Attire

Cosmopolitan Pastiche

Cotton & Wool

For the complete renovation of her 1907 New York apartment, clothing/furnishings designer *Annie Walwyn-Jones* placed front stage center rugs, cushions and needlepoint tapestries by her friend and collaborator *Christine Van der Hurd.*

Walwyn-Jones's own design sensibility is gloriously colorful and slightly whimsical, with an evenhanded attraction to both classical and contemporary styles as well as a generous multicultural mix, so she

sought to merge her home's staid architecture with a dramatic, livable elegance. "I wanted a look that would be ready to go at all times, a flexible space that could translate easily from workspace to kid and dog space to dinner party location," she says.

No wonder she found the answer in Van der Hurd's own marvelous sense of color, texture and scale. For both designers, textiles are a way to build on a theme, level on level, echoing and playing off texture, weave, color, proportion and image in a process they find immensely richer than a flat or printed surface. Also, Van der Hurd's upbeat exuberance corresponds to an extraordinary degree with Walwyn-Jones's own signature — unexpected combinations of colors, varying predicted expectations of scale and, above all, humor.

LEFT *Prominent in the hallway is Christine Van der Hurd's geometric "Recollections" rug of hand-tufted wool and "Floramania," a saffron-and-steel blue wool carpet created with a traditional Indian hand-knotted technique.*

Photography by Rob Gray

OPPOSITE *Christine Van der Hurd's "Tra La La" carpet provides a free-flowing, calligraphic focal point for the living room and a curvaceous counterpoint to the strict geometry of the black-and-white-striped cotton sofa upholstery. "Black and white clarifies the look," says Annie Walwyn-Jones, who turned a chair into another black-and-white punctuation mark against vivid jolts of color in the visually complex silk brocade curtain valances. Exuberant tie-backs in the same brocade are enormous versions of Chinese knotted fabric buttons. Van der Hurd's needlepoint and tapestry pick up the colors in the paintings.*

RIGHT *The bold, graphic bed composition is expressed with a handmade needlepoint covering by Christine Van der Hurd titled "Coquillage: Ocean." Evocative of undersea life, it has a wave-like border.*

Global Ensemble

Cotton, Wool/Cotton, Silk, Nylon/Polyester, Mylar, Leather & Coir

OPPOSITE *Egyptian cotton damask, covering walls and ceiling in the sitting room at LongHouse, is loosely stretched to emphasize its supple, textural quality. The room's international mix includes a Swedish tile stove from Royal Crown European Fireplaces and a game table as well as other contemporary classic wood furniture by Wharton Esherick.*

Photography by Elliott Kaufman

BELOW *In the dining room, sliding fabric panels allow collections to be exchanged for a view of the garden. Two of three tables provide flexible table arrangements as well.*

Photography Courtesy of Jack Lenor Larson

Everywhere one looks, there is sense of craft — craft of myriad cultures from throughout the world. It is as it should be, for this is LongHouse, the Long Island residence of master weaver/textile designer and presi-

dent emeritus of the American Craft Council, *Jack Lenor Larsen.*

Here the beauty of architecture and design never outweighs function, and the function of each space and object, no matter how mundane, is carried out with great beauty — the type of beauty that does not try to take center stage but instead is highly appropriate to and is inspired by the task it serves.

The supremely sensitive balance of art with practicality can be seen in such aspects as Larsen's own living room, dining room and sleeping area. Rather than a bedroom, he has a contemporary platform bed positioned between dressing and sitting rooms. He has designed sliding panels of cloth so that the collections he has chosen to display can be eliminated if a still more visually quiet feeling is desired. And all is arranged so as to emphasize texture, craft and the people who made them rather than to segregate according to market value. Thus, refined silks are mated with obviously hand-hewn woods and elegantly woven linen is joined

with hardy, coarse fiber obtained from the outer husks of coconut shells. The message is that of an enormously cosmopolitan internationalist who also has deep roots in the tribal arts and who is eager to remove the distinction between art and craft.

BELOW *A sea of chrome, canary and lemon yellow ties together two eighteenth-century Chinese black lacquer cabinets with polychrome painting, a seventeenth-century Korean table inlaid with tortoise shell and mother-of-pearl, a gold-leafed Parsons table and a Ming dynasty bronze vase.*

BELOW *The Chens' eighteenth-century Dutch marquetry cabinet, seventeenth-century gilt column and Biedermeier-style chairs are set against the dining room's canvas of reds, blacks and golds. For the drapery, each fixed side hanging was diamond-smocked at the heading and tied back with an invisible brass arm. The length of the drapery, a two-inch drag on the floor, adds to the fullness of each panel.*

OPPOSITE *Each drapery panel was hand-pleated on the yellow stripe and attached to the gilded wood ring, then finished with a bow-tie detail that adds to the curtains' visual height. The hardware is a two-and-a-half-inch spiral fluted pole with turned wood finials in burnished gilt finish.*

An Artful Response

Cotton/Rayon, Cotton/Acrylic, Cotton/Viscose, Cotton/Polyester, Cotton, Leather & Sisal

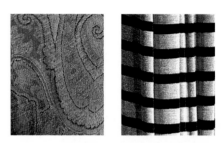

All fabrics in this home's family and dining rooms were selected in response to the major painting in each, creating a delightful as well as soothing interplay of color and line.

Designed by *John* and *Krista Everage* for attorneys Rod Guerra and Carolyn Clark, the youthful California home draws on a mix of Craftsman, Japanese, Mayan and Modern influences. Everage Interior Design was asked to fully furnish the residence in the spirit of these influences but with even further layers of meaning, form and comfort.

The first items selected were the two large paintings, one by Robert Kingston for the dining room, and the other by Avery Faulkner for the family room, both of which were acquired through the Ruth Bachofner Gallery in Santa Monica. Both have great architectural presence, an aspect emphasized in the family room, where a wall was built out to encase the Faulkner piece, making it part of the architecture.

The designers further responded to these artworks by selecting richly woven fabrics with colors, patterns and textures that reflect those in the paintings and actually interpreted the poetic nature of the Kingston work in the dining room's custom-colored and -patterned drapery. At the same time, by allowing the sumptuous drapery to pillow on the floor and placing the highly touchable fabrics on softly curving furniture, the designers were embellishing the architecture's crispness with an all-embracing lilt.

ALL *The dining room's custom drapery fabric carries into the room the tranquil quality established by Robert Kingston's painting, while its horizontal stripe helps to offset the high ceiling. The two high-back end chairs, chosen for the sculptural impact they provide within the simple rectangular room, are upholstered with a commanding tapestry.*

Far Eastern Calm

Linen, Cotton, Sea Grass, Cotton/Rayon, Wool, Silk & Leather

It seemed appropriate that this California home should look out over the Pacific toward Asia, since its owners' interests in food, health and philosophy originate there. Yet the structure itself has little to do with the Pacific Rim feeling they were after, and it was left to **Charles Jacobsen** and **Brad Blair** to create feelings of Oriental tranquility and quiet restfulness with the furnishings alone.

This was not the first time these designers had been presented with such a task. Indeed, the Charles Jacobsen showroom, located in Los Angeles and specializing in fine Japanese antique furnishings, offers a completely meditative experience itself. Yet each project suggests a different solution, and in this one it was the fabrics and related natural window treatments and floorcoverings that best helped redefine the house, softening its scale and enabling it to reemerge with an immense sense of calm.

OPPOSITE A series of contemporary handpainted blue-and-white cotton banners by textile artist Shihoko Fukumoto cued the selection of blue-black linen to cover all upholstery. For throws and pillows the designers used a variety of antique Japanese cottons, their deep indigo, rice paste-resist patterns repeating the technique and color used in the banners' borders. An antique Japanese summer cane floormat (ajiro) defines the seating area.

BELOW A woven cane countertop, illuminated by a small antique Japanese paper lantern (andon), is adorned with an antique Japanese man's cotton sash (saki ori) used as a place mat.

ABOVE A teak banquette with linen cushions, accentuated by antique Japanese blue-and-white cotton for the throw pillows and Japanese floor pillows (zabuton), provides a comfortable platform for a meditation room.

Photography by David Glomb

LEFT A room in which the home's owner practices yoga is intentionally devoid of color. Its design, inspired by colonial India, includes a highly touchable, custom-woven chenille for the daybeds, enhanced by silk bolsters and illuminated by Isamu Noguchi torchiéres, each made from a slender bamboo pole with an unconstructed silk shade.

28

International Evolution

Silk, Cotton & Linen

French-born interior designer **Lisbeth Beise** and her American husband lived in Rio de Janeiro, São Paolo and Tokyo before taking residence in Hong Kong, and it shows. The collectibles that they have amassed from different cultures and which she has arranged form a welcoming, highly spirited potpourri.

The result is a delicate balance of aesthetic and artistic values representing the family's travels while avoiding the sense that these are merely acquired "things." Favorite items usually always find a home, although out of context from each previous home.

"The most difficult part for constantly moving expatriates such as us," says Beise, "is accepting certain pieces for their degree of sentimentality and coziness due to the memories they evoke of past homes and past experiences. The fun is fitting them comfortably among the inevitable new/old purchases of the local country."

Here the challenge was met to a great extent through the use of fabrics, which not only are easily dismountable, but also provide broad, colorful canvases against which to display and connect disparate cultural infusions as well as reflect their countries of origin themselves. In the end, her highly creative solutions combined to make a refreshingly unstudied, untrendy interior and offered a high degree of satisfaction for this designer: the creation of an oasis-like retreat for herself and her family in what is otherwise a very foreign environment.

BELOW In the living room, the designer camouflaged her "first and last attempt at a print on a sofa" by smothering it in various shades and textures of green.

Photography by Do Do Jin Ming

LEFT A diaphanous play of sheer Italian linen, hung on paired rods to create a movable canopy at the dining room skylight, shields the Beises' favorite paintings by Fang from too much light and creates a patchwork of shadows across the walls.

ABOVE *Gloriously glamorous fabrics soften and humanize the grand salon of a palace in Saudi Arabia, with a palette that commenced after Erika Brunson found a rug that looks as if it had been custom-designed for the room's scale, but in fact is an antique Savonnerie.*

LEFT *An overscaled strawberry cotton print, coupled with a small-scaled green-and-off-white cotton plaid, add a delightfully light, outdoor quality to a latticed garden room.*

ABOVE *With an eighteenth-century modified flamestitch in wool, taken from an eighteenth-century archive but recolored, Erika Brunson combines a solid combed cotton in a cornsilk hue to add visual weight.*

RIGHT *A solid sunshine yellow cotton twill adds a sense of continuity to an area that is enhanced by curved glass and geometrical shapes in the marble floor.*

OPPOSITE *Expanses of solid-colored silk juxtaposed with wool needlepoint and flamestitch provide variations on the green and gold theme.*

ABOVE *A classic eighteenth-century documentary ikat, of watermarked pure silk in yellow, sage and mauve, is draped from the ceiling to the floor.*

RIGHT *A cashmere print, crimson custom-dyed leather and a classic watermarked ikat mohair interplay with a collection of ethnic garments in an air of festive celebration.*

Photography courtesy of Erika Brunson Design Associates

Hermès Fashion Show

Silk, Raffia, Cotton, Wool, Leather & Sisal

Mike Moore had long been tempted to design a room with some of the splendid fabrics available in the fashion industry and, when making over this library, he did it.

Chairs are dressed with opulent Hermès saddle and handbag leathers. Built-in benches sport Hermès horse blankets. A pair of Louis XV-style fauteuils juxtapose raffia with Hermès hand-screened silk scarves, more of which adorn the pillows. And an Hermès daybed is even draped with an Hermès mink throw.

The effect is pure luxury, but **Mike Moore** is quick to point out that it makes good sense, too. "For people who feel that wearing their fur coats is no longer politically correct, recycling them into throws is the perfect answer," he explains. "And as for scarves, 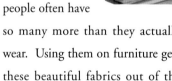 people often have so many more than they actually wear. Using them on furniture gets these beautiful fabrics out of the closet and into the limelight."

THIS PAGE *To brighten what was originally an oppressively dark room, Mike Moore lightened the walls with paint, covered the floors with honey-colored sisal, and dressed the furniture in scarves from Hermès.*

Photography by John Vaughan

ABOVE *Chairs are upholstered with opulent Hermès saddle and handbag leathers.*

RIGHT *Built-in benches sport Hermès horse blankets.*

English Cottage Snuggery

Cotton, Silk, Rayon, Cotton/Rayon & Linen

This cottage on a stud horse farm in the English countryside seems the same as it might have been when built more than two hundred years ago. Its charming flint, stone and brick facade seems more bent on beckoning

guests to come in from Wiltshire's frequently chill weather than on impressing them, and its interior, scaled low and of snug proportion, aimed more at immediately accessible warmth and comfort than formality. What a surprise to learn that it has just been completely redesigned and furnished by Honolulu designer *Allison A. Holland.*

"Because of the home's cottage-like nature, it was important to not overdo," she says.

Yet because of the area's shivery dampness, Holland deemed it equally important to achieve a cozy, inviting atmosphere by using the brightest, warmest colors, with as many patterns and kinds of fabric as possible. In the living room, even the antique blackamoor and tapestry sconces were selected for their contribution of color and pattern. And in the master bedroom, in which the overall design is as formal as the house would allow, the bed treatment's full-blown floral pattern is balanced by a solid lemon yellow stretching the length of the walls to which it is connected by a sparsely patterned paper at the ceiling.

It was due to Holland's great sensitivity to pattern and color that each of the rooms became excitingly individual and even highly sophisticated without spoiling the home's basic character of thoroughly likable simplicity.

LEFT *A charming flint, stone and brick exterior dictated that the interiors of this eighteenth-century stone cottage on a horse farm in Wiltshire evidence a similarly accessible charm.*

BELOW *To ward off the chill winters of the English countryside, the warmest colors in as many patterns as possible were chosen to achieve a cozy atmosphere.*

ABOVE & RIGHT *In the master bedroom, the intensity of the major floral pattern required art and furniture to be equally dark and intense. The flat lemon yellow walls were enhanced with a simple white boiserie molding to provide the necessary "wake-up call" the client requested. The sparse pattern of the paper used at the ceiling became the necessary transition between the plain walls and the bed treatment incorporating a twenty-six-screen cotton chintz.*

Photography by David Livingston

43

Shall We Dance?

Cotton & Wool

Traditional and contemporary, embellished and simplified — a variety of feelings go into the cosmopolitan mix of **Sandra Nunnerley's** design and the taste of her international clientele as well. She has lived and worked around the globe and so have they, and they usually like their homes to reflect it.

For this nursery in an Austrian home, the parents wanted their daughter to grow from infancy to adulthood in a sophisticated room, surrounded by fine continental antiques and lilting, not cute, embellishments. Nunnerley's answer was to shun traditional pink and blue and instead combine soft reds, yellows and dove grays for all fabrics, culminating in a towering canopy treatment beautifully made up by a Paris workshop and easily accommodated under the room's twelve-foot-high ceiling. The iron Empire campaign bed, formerly black, has been painted red. Other treasures include an eighteenth-century chest and table and an heirloom bassinet. The result definitely seems inspired by Strauss waltzes, not Mother Goose.

ALL *Throughout this highly cosmopolitan room designed not only for an infant but for the young lady she will become, chintz prints are combined with solids, while an unglazed cotton covers the walls.*

Photography by Jaime Ardiles-Arce

Evening Dress

Sisal, Viscose Modacrylic, Cotton, Silk & Wool

As necessity is the mother of invention, challenge is often the mother of great creativity. The gauntlet thrown to **Meryl Hare** was the room she was assigned to decorate for an exhibition at Australia's historic Lindesay

House in Sydney. Rooms were drawn by ballot, and she drew the basement — completely below ground level and made of sandstone. Furthermore, due to the heritage listing of Lindesay, no permanent structures or fittings could be added to amend the restricted, windowless space. All furnishings had to be fixed to existing details with no damage to the walls.

With her typical, thoroughly professional never-you-mind attitude, Hare immediately set about emphasizing the negative as if it were a positive. Titling her room "Room with No View," she decorated it as an evening salon, the sort of cozy, inviting place guests would gather after the theater for port and conversation. Despite the introduction of a strong contemporary painting and high-tech lights, the overall feeling is traditional, with strong contrasts of color and texture and a highly eclectic mix of furniture providing the warmth she was after.

Many a basement room could be helped by such a strategy.

ALL *Antique black-lacquered kimono chests, a French Provincial table, a Chinese chest, Indian boat prows and an antiqued Georgian-style screen combine with richly colored and textured fabrics to create an eclectic warmth in a windowless space.*

Photography by Richard Waugh

French Liberties

Silk, Viscose/Linen/Cotton, Suedecloth, Wool, Rayon/Cotton, Linen, Cotton, Sisal & Leather

Located in one of New York City's most prestigious prewar buildings, this apartment had been owned by many illustrious people but, during the evolution of time, had been severely neglected. Therefore the premise of the project, undertaken by **Joseph Braswell**, was that of restoration as well as decoration. However, it was not exactly a precise restoration.

"The 'bones' were French, but certain liberties were taken to give the environment a sense of 'today,'" says the designer.

Yet even in rooms most contemporized, the careful selection of appropriate fabrics and surfaces creates a true sense of classical French authenticity with reference to classic motifs. Indeed, throughout this splendid space, the owners' goal — to be able to entertain their guests with style and grace — was realized more than expected.

LEFT *The walls of the dining room have been upholstered in an aubergine matte silk faille to temper any acoustical problems resulting from the expansive marble floor. The sheer undercurtains are illuminated from behind to give a sense of sunlight all evening long.*

OPPOSITE *The simplicity of the guest room's blue-and-white color scheme and the purposeful elimination of wall art enhance the dramatic lit de polonaise bed treatment, composed of a modest cotton block print echoed by the upholstered walls' Provenç al striped linen.*

Photography by Norman McGrath

RIGHT *The drawing room is graced with early-eighteenth-century painted boiserie accented with finely burnished gold leaf which cued the coloring of all fabrics — golden velour, cream-and-gold brocade, pale gray moiré, and citron glove leather. The early-nineteenth-century Aubusson rug serves as a foundation for the salon's golden glow.*

City Suiting

Delight to Hand and Eye

Silk, Cotton, Wool, Linen/Cotton, Camel's Hair & Sisal

To interior designer **Marjorie Shushan**, the sense of touch is as important as sight. In her New York apartment, she combined nubby cottons, gossamer-light silks, sleek gold-threaded sari fabric, coarse camel's hair, polished

cotton and deeply piled matelassé.

Though one would never know it, this was a quick job, the speed necessitated by having a mere five weeks to move from her former home into a new one, thirty-five floors up and next-door to the Museum of Modern Art in New York. Foregoing her usually more permanent architectural rearranging, she decided to count on the stupendous view for most of the spectacle and used fabric, some of it taken from the drapery in her former dwelling and reused here in other forms, to camouflage certain aspects or divert the eye.

"I felt confident that the warmth of my color and the richness of my fabrics would compensate for the lack of architectural detailing," she says.

By move-in day, each delightful room truly did feel as good as it looked.

ABOVE *Looking out over some of New York's most illustrious buildings, black leather chairs and a pedestal table are framed by silk taffeta drapery rather than the massive structural columns it hides.*

Photography by Billy Cunningham

RIGHT *The range of hues complements the parchment color of the painted walls as well as the natural sisal flooring, both used throughout the apartment to create a soothing, visibly seamless background. Black accents anchor the pervasive beige.*

ABOVE *In the master bed-*
room, a massive canopy of
parchment-colored cotton
linen creates a room-within-
a-room. At its foot is a Louis
XVI-style bench covered
with a complementary light-
weight cream-colored hounds-
tooth wool.

OPPOSITE *Black moldings*
unify the black-on-tan
checkerboard tweed used for
drapery and bed treatment in
the guest bedroom, a neutral
scheme uninterrupted by the
designer's collection of nine-
teenth-century Chinese prints.

Planes in Space

Leather, Silk, Wool & Stainless Steel

Similar to the way in which they treat all architectural elevations of their classically contemporary interiors, **Donald D. Powell** and **Robert D. Kleinschmidt** treat upholstered pieces, drapery and all other fabric and leather applications as planes in space.

For a study in an apartment in Chicago's 860 Lakeshore Drive cooperative, designed by Ludwig Mies van der Rohe in 1949, Powell used leather to define the sleek geometry of ottomans and chairs.

Steel mesh turns floor-to-ceiling panels into glimmering, vertical rectangles. Silk drapery provides a comforting sense of enclosure while framing the view. And tautly upholstered wool converts a seating unit into an exercise in clarity of material.

"It is challenging to use fabrics in so many ways to define forms and still express the innate qualities of the materials," says Powell.

Such an emphasis on maintaining the integrity of each material and the distinction between them can be seen throughout Powell/Kleinschmidt's work and is vital to their overriding "planes in space" concept.

ABOVE *Various wools, silks and leather read like an exercise in clarity of materials that seem to float individually over the white marble floor.*

Photography by Jon Miller, Hedrich-Blessing

RIGHT *When visiting a silk scarf factory in Italy, Donald D. Powell became fascinated with the stainless steel mesh used in the silk-screen process and decided to use a stainless steel version to wrap the floor-to-ceiling particleboard panels, which conceal a coat/wine/stereo storage unit.*

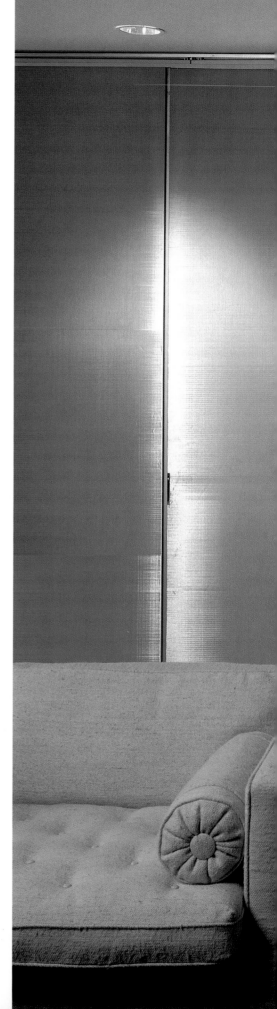

Indoor Heaven

Cotton/Lurex, Rayon, Wool, Leather & Mohair

An ethereal golden fabric ceiling continues inside the warm exterior hue of this contemporary Italian villa. Designed by the project's architects, **James Olson** and **Tom Kundig** of Olson/Sundberg, and interior designer

Mary Siebert, the unusual ceiling, which also hides lighting, heating and stereo apparatus, is definitely as important aesthetically as it is functional.

"The idea for the fabric ceiling was a contemporary version of a Renaissance fresco depicting the sky and clouds to visually expand a ceiling beyond its actual structure," says Olson. "In addition, besides concealing visually distracting mechanical systems, it helped diminish the acoustical problems that often result from rooms having as many hard surfaces as in this residence."

Used for all first-floor ceilings of the home designed for a prominent art collector and located on Lake Washington, Seattle, rectangles of gold lamé and sheer rayon are set within painted wood frames. The fabrics' shimmering luminosity across the fourteen-foot-high ceilings picks up the warm wheat color of the villa's exterior stucco and also offers a sympathetic response to the lively translucency of the client's extensive art glass collection. This use of fabric to solve a functional problem in such an unusually beautiful and creative manner makes it seem like a specially commissioned work of art itself.

LEFT *The warm hues used for the exterior of this Seattle residence are much more indicative of the Mediterranean than the Pacific Northwest and are continued on all interior finishes, furnishings and fabrics.*

Photography by Michael Jensen

BELOW *The rug in the family room, designed on a computer by Seattle artist Carl T. Chew to look like koi swimming in a pond, emphasizes further the idea that the fabric ceiling tiles are actually golden clouds in the sky.*

RIGHT *The pattern of the slate-and-tile floor helps to define smaller areas within the space, necessarily expansive to properly display the owner's many sizable works of art.*

ABOVE *Each ceiling tile is a two-part composition of a central cotton/Lurex gold lamé rectangle covered by a larger rectangle of sheer rayon, which slightly masks the gold lamé's reflective quality.*

ABOVE *To give a sense of human scale to the mammoth living/dining area, as well as baffle sound and hide electrical and heating systems, cloud-like panels of fabric were hung over the entire first floor's interior.*

Japanese Home, Western Dress

Cotton, Silk/Viscose & Wool

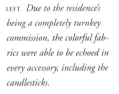

European and American plaids, stripes and prints took the place of structural reconfigurations to make this home in Chiba prefecture, near Tokyo, approximate the client's wish for it to be "the most Western house in Japan." President of a software company with many U.S. customers, he had handed the turn-key job to **John David Edison** of Toronto, who, in lieu of architectural changes forbidden by the Japanese developer, relied on strongly colored and patterned fabrics to create the desired atmosphere.

Drapery was used to soften the architecture, while carpet and upholstery became canvases on which to insert strong plays of hue and pattern into the voluminous, 7,200-square-foot residence with double-height first-floor living and dining areas. The result is a warmly inviting environment in which furniture and accessories have been carefully placed to create a balance of old and new and a feeling that the international assemblage is composed of items collected abroad by the client himself.

"If the heart of an interior lies in its structural presence, its soul is less tangible," says Edison. "It grows from an understanding of architecture, is shaped by ingenuity and personal dreams. It reaches beyond construction to the interplay of design and detail, of bold gestures, rich textures and fresh impressions. In all of this, color and fabrics are key. They create an architecture of their own."

LEFT *Due to the residence's being a completely turnkey commission, the colorful fabrics were able to be echoed in every accessory, including the candlesticks.*

Photography by Isao Aihara

BELOW & OPPOSITE *Located in an exclusive, expensive development near Tokyo, such residences as this are sold with one of several interior options. In this case, the owner asked Canadian designer John David Edison to change almost everything and to make it brighter and warmer. Edison's solution came via color and pattern in fabrics and carpet.*

Well-Ordered Calm

Polyester, Cotton, Silk, Leather & Wool

There is an orderly precision to rooms designed by **Arthur de Mattos Casas**, which makes comparisons to fine art inescapable. Composed of striking contemporary furnishings that are all treated as works of art, the rooms  themselves are edited like some masterful contemporary canvas in which color, form and scale have been intensely studied.

"In my work I've always tried to point up the design of each object and each piece of furniture," he explains. "According to the weight and importance I want to give to a particular piece of furniture, the fabric is regarded as more or less important. I am not keen on using color compositions as mere decoration."

In each of the three residences shown here, Casas has used fabric with greatest care to not overwhelm either the rooms' other aspects or their pervasive sense of calm that is this Brazilian designer's trademark. The reserved yet commanding strength he has achieved is impressive.

BELOW *Arthur de Mattos Casas planned this room so as not to interfere with his client's own repertoire of small collections, which the designer was asked to edit and organize. Instead he selected fabrics carefully, for the most part letting them provide a neutral background of black or beige, yet also using them to periodically echo the primary colors found in the rest of the assemblage.*

ABOVE *For a lounge at the "Casa Cor" showcase house in São Paulo, a monochromatic color scheme creates a mood of tranquility. The wall treatment was created by artist Herman Tacasey and is made of plaster, sand and cement on which he drew with charcoal.*

LEFT *For an elegant yet casual environment for a young couple, an emphasis on neutral tones is enlivened by a few strokes of red.*

Photography by Tuca Reinés

Point of View

Silk/Polyester, Cotton, Cotton/Silk & Linen Silk

"An environment should be the extension of one's being," says **Lorraine Crockford**, an interior designer who has a master's degree in clinical psychology. Her design of this second home for a couple from Japan exemplifies how she herself follows what she preaches by trying to

truly understand who her clients really are.

Her clients wanted a sensitive expression of warm yet intimate and peaceful hospitality — even though the space itself, located in a high-rise building in Los Angeles, had an unlived-in coldness that regulations prevented being altered architecturally. However, the condominium did have a major

LEFT *Floral arrangements by Lois Howard and personal possessions such as the obi and antique hanging scroll painting (*kakejiku*) reflect the Japanese heritage of the people who live here and further emphasize their desire for their surroundings to express a quiet harmony.*

Photography by Anthony Peres

BELOW, OPPOSITE & OVERLEAF *Subtle variations in texture and materials, including travertine and white-washed oak as well as various fabrics, bring great interest to the residence despite its completely neutral palette.*

attraction — its view and quality of light, especially the way it changes throughout the day. It was this, then, on which Crockford focused, and she did this by seemingly de-emphasizing everything else, from the color palette to the number of possessions. Yet "seemingly" is an appropriate modifier, for the careful composition of a few rich fabrics, variously textured via subtly differentiated weaves, becomes a sea of white that, in fact, is an undeniable summons for all to be calm and to drink in the cityscape below.

Indeed, the combination of this quietly neutral oasis and the highly edited selection

of a few prized items — from an antique Japanese scroll painting that had been a wedding gift, to the exquisite Japanese-style floral arrangements by Lois Howard — make the view within the home every bit as enchanting as the view beyond.

Modern Design 1890-1990

Loft-Style Ingenuity

Silk-Screened Paper

No matter how much those living in one-room lofts like their homes' sense of openness, sooner or later they usually find they need a sense of demarcation between areas as well. Architect/designer **Geoffrey Scott** has faced the challenge so frequently that by now he has created a series of dividers so visually intriguing that they are no less than works of art — and they all incorporate silk-screened fabric techniques.

To separate adjacent living spaces, he used fabrics in the silk-screen and pattern-making process, then screened the designs onto burlap, Mylar, wood and metal, as well as the paper shown here, and ... voila! An ingenious collection of one-of-a-kind dividers and panels!

"The use of fabrics permits me to create expressive, abstract or storytelling patterns and to reproduce them in a multitude of colors on a variety of materials," says Scott. "Planes which define or divide interior space are then endowed with meaning."

ABOVE *The pastel organic grid motif has been silk-screened onto soft-white vellum paper with a light turquoise ink.*

RIGHT *Hanging silk-screened paper separates a bedroom from an adjacent sitting area and provides a grid of calm translucence as well.*

Photography by Hugo Rojas

Embellished Music

Cotton, Silk, Jute & Wool

A suite of rooms — entry, living room and alcove — were all to reflect the importance of music to this family. The baby grand piano as well as the cello are heard and not just seen in this Sydney, Australia, home.

The design brief of Hare & Klein partner **Meryl Hare** was to create a rich, inviting environment, yet one that would not be intimidating to the family's children when practicing or performing. She also was to use the existing plantation shutter windows and doors, painted a gray beige hue to match the walls, as well as retain the somber gray carpet. In addition, her clients wanted no floral patterns. Her answer, especially since this room faces south, a home's darker side in the Southern Hemisphere, was to introduce a subtle variety of fabrics that would blend with the existing tones, yet bring warmth and interest to the rooms.

To harmonize with the existing shell, Hare selected a variety of neutral-colored fabrics, including damask, shadowbox and hand-printed silks, one of them designed with a "Mozart" theme that ideally symbolizes the rooms' intent. This was made into a screen to help overcome the echo effect caused by the many hard surfaces. Hare also introduced dark fabrics in indigo, black and red to balance the visual weight of the black piano (in alcove, not shown). This eclectic mix was further accented with a collection of French antiques.

BELOW *Dark accents in a sea of lighter neutrals begin at the entry.*

Photography by Richard Waugh

OPPOSITE & RIGHT *The eclectic mix of fabrics — hand-woven silks, unusual cotton prints and handmade jute trimmings — makes the reserved color palette seem anything but static.*

Sky-High Euphoria

Cotton, Silk, Wool, Wool/Silk & Leather

Vintage properties need not always summon forth grand gestures. Architect **Emanuela Frattini Magnusson** tempered the respect she felt for the bones of this prewar apartment in New York City with a hefty dose of tongue-in-cheek daring.

"The owners, a young couple with two small children, didn't want to just mimic tradition," says Magnusson. "They were more interested in marrying the existing architecture with their own way of life and tastes, which are decidedly more unconventional."

She and **Oscar Shamamian** of Fergusson Murray & Shamamian, Architects enhanced this home's period feeling with their carefully executed cabinetry and ironwork, but then she threw historic prudence to the winds by infusing every room with a sense of levity.

Carla Weisberg's textile designs play visual trickery in the dining room and dance a jig in the library, and Frattini's own carpet design runs up the stairs with polka dots. These seemingly serendipitous "happenings," combined with the dining room's 360-degree Manhattan scenic by artist Paul Osborne, make one feel more than a bit lightheaded.

LEFT *The hues commenced in the dining room continue right up the stairs.*

Photography by Nola Lopez

OPPOSITE *The dining room's colorful, geometric fabric design is reinterpreted in the library's carpet.*

BELOW *In the dining room, various colors on The Knoll Group's chairs pick up the playful beat that is further enhanced by Carla Weisberg's stenciled stripes.*

Eloquent Layering

Silk, Linen, Mohair, Cotton, Rayon, Wool & Leather

Selecting the right fabrics for a room is almost a science to **Mars** and **Ronn Jaffe**, so exacting are they in searching for the precisely right color and fiber palette.

"For the most part, we are purists," says Mars. "Our primary interest is in subtlety of hue, so we are more inclined to use neutrals and depend for interest on the interplay of light and dark. When we do use vivid color, we usually introduce it in small objects, such as in pillows, ottomans, accessories and art."

For the most part, however, these designers lean toward monochromatic schemes and, by their brilliant use of just one color — interpreted in exquisitely varied hues and textures — they create as much interest as if they had used every color in the rainbow.

RIGHT *Durability and comfort as well as aesthetic appeal made mohair and an intaglio-patterned rayon the fabrics of choice for the upholstery. Two unexpected notes, the window treatment's blue leather harlequin trim and beams stenciled with biomorphic shapes, provide whimsy.*

ABOVE *The bold geometric design of a lush wool area rug unifies this living room's equally strong furniture forms, their weighty sculptured shapes upholstered with correspondingly hefty mohair and chenille. Both rug and furniture were designed by Ronn Jaffe as works of art.*

RIGHT *Blackout curtains, fabricated of puddle-length silk scrim over heavy cotton, are hung from hand-forged iron rods to provide a dramatic backdrop for entertainment as well as conceal this room's awkward window placement.*

Photography by Mark Weiland

Pieces of Sky

Canvas, Linen, Cotton & Wool

The painter's canvas is not usually thought of as a textile surface, but in this particular instance, the canvas is the medium that expresses architect **Rand Elliott's** concept, "pieces of sky."

Four large canvas panels have been painted by artist Lammy Weisman in hues of yellow, blue, pink and violet, representing the

moods of the Oklahoma sky stretching over the Lawton home of doctors Jack and Rosemary Bellino-Hall. Except in the bathrooms, where windows looking toward the distant Wichita Mountains and "real" sky were deemed sufficient, these panels expand the view and provide the color in all areas of the house. Otherwise, the serenely pared-down environment is completely neutral save for a few sparsely placed, jewel-toned upholstered pieces and collection of Fiesta Ware pottery that, in this setting, seem like smaller "pieces of sky."

For a minimalist environment for two busy professionals who like nothing better than getting away in their private airplane, this artful use of textile and color provides a similar sense of soaring in air.

LEFT *The entry floor, inlaid with bands of walnut, harmonizes in feeling with the dining room's heirloom furniture. Both are set in high relief against Lammy Weisman's lustrous artworks, the result of his sealing each canvas with gesso, then sanding it, and then repeating the process several times before applying satin-finish wall paint.*

Photography by Bob Shimer, Hedrich-Blessing

BELOW *The large, flowing spaces resulting from Rand Elliott's remodel of a 1954 home for two doctors who are also pilots are tied together by four painted canvas panels, reflecting the owners' preference for the airy serenity they find when flying.*

BELOW *In the living room, a modular sofa upholstered with linen can variously take advantage of views of the fireplace, of one of Lammy Weisman's "pieces of sky" or the sweeping vista west toward the Wichita Mountains.*

RIGHT *In the master bedroom, hues of the "pieces of sky" are echoed by the cotton bedspread and a chair upholstered in wool.*

Utter Opulence

Silk, Cotton, Cotton/Linen, & Cotton/Rayon

His look has been dubbed "opulent California," a description that amuses designer *Reginald Adams* even though he says he can see the reason for it. Yet one has only to experience his particular type of opulence to realize that

rooms he has created are governed by an intense sense of restraint. His work is grand without being ponderous, and no matter how many elements he uses, juxtaposing smooth silks with rough-textured cottons and natural stone material with intricately manipulated pieces, an open airiness rather than a suffocating overabundance prevails.

"I push the dressiness and number of decorative elements right up to the edge, trying to stay just this side of being overdone and cluttered," notes Adams. "To achieve this, it often is quite evident to me that the selection of neutral, light colors will augment rather than interrupt the feeling of spacious continuity I seek. But it takes an enormous amount of planning to get the balance just right."

BELOW *A high sense of dramatic opulence is achieved through a congenial seating area of soft and overstuffed upholstery and a combination of textures, including the woven cotton for the tented ceiling and walls and the nubbier cotton weave on the furniture.*

OPPOSITE *"I use textures and rich fabrics but not that much color, because I seem to tire of anything stronger than neutrals," explains Reginald Adams. "A room should be beautiful based solely on its scale and the shape of the pieces within it."*

ABOVE *Commenting on the master bedroom in his own home, Adams says, "I simply wanted the look to be dramatic without being formal. The interplay of the fabrics' beautiful textures and sheens was all that was needed."*

Photography by Mary E. Nichols

Formal Wear

Silk, Wool, Cotton, Cotton/Rayon, Rayon, Linen, Suede, Leather & Horsehair

The highly elegant yet luxuriously comfortable feeling that has become the signature of **Mark Enos** and his late partner **Richard L. Mayhew** was fulfilled beyond expectation in these spaces created for two design showcases, the master bedroom of a Bel Air mansion and an imagined New York penthouse.

The master bedroom was designed in response to the 1920s Moorish-style home, an exotic and glamorous haven that might have been prepared as a retreat for a fabled movie star. The sparing use of color focuses attention on the home's inherently dramatic architecture. Ebony floors, beeswax-polished and Venetian-plastered walls and an abundance of white linen create a backdrop for a collection of antiques, contemporary furnishings and art.

The New York penthouse was conceived as a space that would also serve as a design studio, its hardwood floors and fabric-covered walls setting the mood for an elevated atmosphere that would not only uplift one's creative hours, but also be appropriate for receiving clientele. An eclectic mixture of fine antiques and contemporary custom-designed upholstery and drapery provided the understated answer.

LEFT *A Squeak Carnwarth painting serves as backdrop for a plant set into a Spanish brazier and a linen-upholstered chaise. An antique pillow rich with gold thread and tapestry adds to the ambience.*

BELOW *The curved rails and antique columns set on metal bases were all created to give the bed scale and grandeur.*

Photography by John Vaughan

OPPOSITE *A gilded, celestial feeling emanates from an abundance of yellow silk, white linen and beeswax-polished Venetian-plastered walls, creating a magnificent backdrop for an interesting mix of antiques, contemporary furnishings and modern art.*

Photography by Michael Arden

LEFT & OVERLEAF *Richly woven fabrics, suede and horsehair bring a lustrous, textural feeling to a studio. Their hues are inspired by the fine antique Persian area rug. The contemporary, patternless weave of the reversible drapery fabric incorporates two different colors of silk thread to give it an iridescent quality.*

Photography by David Glomb

Traditional Habits

Pacific Symphony

Leather, Silk, Wool, Cotton/Linen, Rayon, Rayon/Cotton & Cotton

In this grand residence overlooking the Pacific in Palos Verdes, California, the scale of traditionally inspired millwork is far greater than normal. Substantially sized accessories hold court in unexpected places. And the

simplified color palette is endlessly reinterpreted through softly upholstered walls and elegantly plush furniture so that its calmness soothes but never bores. It is through such techniques, gained from their experience in hotel design, that James Northcutt Associates' *James Northcutt* and *Darrell Schmitt* control vast spaces and enliven them.

Within the Mediterranean look established here by architect *Edward Carson Beall* at the request of their clients, Northcutt and Schmitt were able to influence the entire interior development through a variety of materials, including custom millwork designs and special wood-and-stone flooring. The Mediterranean influence was layered with additional interior design references preferred by the clients, such as English antiques, blue-and-white por-

celains, furnishings with a lightly Bavarian flavor, and both European and Oriental art. The evidence resounds with every note of this balanced and proportioned orchestration. Each is a carefully chosen element in a totally harmonious whole.

ABOVE LEFT *The exterior architecture, which is northern Mediterranean in feeling without belaboring a truly specific theme, set the tone for the entire interior.*

Photography by Mary E. Nichols

ABOVE & RIGHT *A soft pistachio gives a restful tranquility to the master bedroom, while the russet that predominates in some public rooms downstairs is given play in the chintz bed drapery.*

ABOVE *Crystal, porcelain and mahogany gleam amid the dining room's sea of silk, some of it tied with black grosgrain.*

RIGHT *The upholstered walls throughout become a soft foil to an eclectic mix of art and artifacts that one immediately identifies as a personal collection rather than just decoration.*

RIGHT & FAR RIGHT *Color selection and texture add to the overall mood and ambience of each space, as in the central foyer's seventeenth-century Belgian needlepoint tapestry, the soft leather on St. Denis Design's bench, and the rich russet wool moiré wall upholstery. "The softness of upholstered walls gives a refinement and plushness to wall surfaces not possible with paint or paper," says James Northcutt.*

LEFT *The guest bedroom's completely neutral palette exudes freshness, while a variety of textures and fabric treatments prevents it from even coming close to bland.*

French Normandy Comfort

Cotton, Cotton/Rayon, Cotton Silk, Linen/Cotton & Wool

Long before ground was broken, designers **Marjorie A. Bedell** and **Lawrence G. Laughlin** worked with Charles and Joann Anderson on developing interiors for the French Normandy-style home the Andersons intended to build in Pasadena, California. By the end of the process, fabrics, predominantly eighteenth-century French and English document prints, their colors and designs governed by the floorcoverings, came to play a highly important part in creating the desired sense of comfort and charm.

"We start each room with the floorcovering, as its size alone makes it the pacesetter for the other colors, designs and textures to be used in the same space," says Bedell. "In the Anderson residence, the dining room's fine, semi-antique Oriental carpet lends an atmosphere of warmth, high style and fine art appropriate to the home's architecture and governed that room's fabrics, inspired by document prints and weaves. Similarly, in the master bedroom and bath, we chose fabrics that would sing with the light, petit point carpet underfoot."

OPPOSITE *The designers draped the French doors with a country French polished cotton over a linen/cotton lace sheer. However, this same combination at the arched recessed window would have made the room too dark, so the sheer was used alone in a sunburst design.*

RIGHT *In the master bath, the bedroom's drapery fabric is repeated in a tied-back panel for separation between the tub and dressing area.*

Photography by Anthony Peres

ABOVE *Shirred fabric walls originated in eighteenth-century Europe to cover rain-stained plaster and keep out drafts, but it is their ability to project warmth and tradition that makes them a preferred decorative technique of Bedell-Laughlin & Associates today.*

LEFT *In the dining room, the fabrics were selected to complement the antique Laver-Kirman carpet which covers most of the floor, including a multicolored tapestry on the side dining chairs, rose chenille on the host and hostess chairs, and an airy French document print at the windows.*

Reinterpreting the Past

Silk, Cotton, Linen/Cotton, Cotton/Rayon, Silk/Cotton, Wool & Leather

In the design of architects **Carlos** and **Gerard Pascal**, fabric can truly be seen as a home's second skin whose softness and warmth make it a welcome and ever-present companion, and whose limitless variations make it an ideal tool with which to represent individual traditions and culture.

"We dress in it, sleep on it, walk on it, dry with it, cry on it, shade with it," says Gerard Pascal. "And through the use of different fibers, dying techniques, printing, painting and weaves, it offers the opportunity to express character and style in any way imaginable."

In these two residences in Mexico, what Pascal Arquitectos conceived was a sense of period without being precisely literal. For a neoclassical feeling in one and the character of an old European mansion in the other, an array of diverse and sumptuous fabrics turned their ideas into reality.

LEFT *A floral motif against a rich yellow ground warms a classical foyer.*

BELOW LEFT *A rich combination of leather, linen and cotton is enhanced by both printed and painted spiral leaf motifs.*

BELOW *The soft colors of an antique Tabriz are picked up in a variety of textures.*

OPPOSITE *In a penthouse high above Mexico City, a neoclassical feeling is created through the use of materials associated with the Spanish colonial style.*

Photography by Victor Benitez

RIGHT & FAR RIGHT *A crescendo of lustrous red and gold salutes David Ligare's painted landscape.*

OPPOSITE *Lilting hues of gold, green, peach and lavender play a light symphony around the symmetrically poised dining room.*

LEFT *Floral designs in cotton and painted metal give a lightly romantic touch to a bedroom for two young girls.*

A Feminine Ambience

Linen, Cotton, Silk, Wool & Acetate

LEFT & OPPOSITE *The same English cotton used for the bedroom continues at the shirred ceiling and walls of the veranda beyond. Here, delicate sheers instead of the heavily lined drapery used elsewhere allow the room to be filled with light.*

Photography by Robert Emmett Bright and Allesandro De Crignis

This Italian designer likes houses that give the impression that they have not been decorated. Nothing in her own design seems forced, or compromised, or too perfect.

Daniela Leusch, who resides in Milan and grew up in a home that itself was highly sophisticated, was discovered at an early age to have a good eye. Soon she gained even greater familiarity with fine old furniture and fabrics during a three-year period when she worked for Ciga Hotels. Then she commenced designing on her own, bringing her special touch to villas on the French coast, a chalet in the mountains, a palace in Venice and urban apartments, two of which are shown here.

In the apartment of Countess Domitella Gerli in the heart of Milan's fashion district, her intention was to create a smooth, feminine ambience for a young romantic lady, a place where she could feel protected. The choice of fabrics, always important in Leusch's traditional and livable environments, was influenced here by the client's art collection.

ABOVE *In the living room of Countess Domitella Gerli, green printed velvet and a cotton print wallcovering provide a compatible neoclassical surrounding for the subjects of the commanding works of art. The cushions are covered with pieces of old French Aubusson carpets.*

For the master bedroom in Daniela Leusch's own entrancing home, the king-size bed and cushions present a meadow of old French laces beneath a fountain of thick beige silk taffeta as baldachin. The walls are upholstered with a linen floral print on which Leusch added painted stripes echoing those of the drapery and about which the blue and pink flowers are entwined in a feminine embrace.

OPPOSITE & BELOW *To intensify the traditional feeling conveyed by the nineteenth-century painting,* Lady with a Cushion *by Vigée Lebrun, as well as a seventeenth-century Italian bronze, all walls are upholstered over a felt underlayer and curtains are heavily lined.*

ABOVE *In the designer's own home, a protective baldechin of thick beige silk taffeta frames a seventeenth-century French painting from the Atelier of Watteau, and together they provide a lilting backdrop for an abundance of antique French lace.*

Timeless Classics

Silk, Linen & Suede

Marcie Vesel Bronkar imbues rooms with the same subtle marriage of color, texture and classic designs that she brings to her Home Couture line of printed textiles — interpretations of historical documents and

new hand-blocked prints in gloriously soft, almost indefinable hues. Both reflect her vision of fabric as a means to compose environments that are warm and reassuring but quietly discreet.

"I'm inspired to design more for the negative than the positive space," she says. "To me, whether one is designing fabrics or the entire interior, the main challenge is to create something substantial without being obvious."

Bronkar explains: "Designing textiles is a passionate process. I found that there is not a lot of effort or planning in the creative development of an idea. One must be considerably familiar with modern and historical technical capabilities in addition to upholding a strict quality code. The remainder lies in the designer's contribution.

"This is where the substantial question arises. Not being too obvious is simply the result of blending inherent style with respect for and utilization of existing surroundings. Good design should act more as a comfortable, subtle way of satisfying our aesthetic and functional needs.

"The use of casual throws, slipcovers and fabric-covered walls adds an enormous warmth and substance to a room and tends to act as a backdrop rather than just a highly visible decorative object or addition."

OPPOSITE *"It's a challenge to create something substantial but not obvious," says Bronkar, who likes to let the substance of richly textured fabric speak through muted tones.*

BELOW *To complement the French Normandy style of the home of architect Jann C. Williams, Bronkar custom designed hand-printed velvet for the drapery and lined it with a pleated silk.*

LEFT *Hand-printed natural linen used for a window seat is accented with vintage pillows. Casual throws draped on Danish leather chairs are of suede, linen and velvet. The sheers are Moroccan linen.*

Photography by Anthony Peres

ABOVE *A faded eighteenth-century map of Paris is complemented by the similar aged hues of Bronkar's velvets.*

RIGHT *On a Venetian pewter chair, Bronkar has draped antiqued velvet with still more velvet and used an eighteenth-century French wood block document on antiqued velvet for the curtains, creating a montage of whisper-soft hues.*

LEFT *Velvets for drapes, chairs and throws bring warmth and texture to a library, their well-worn hues achieved by the use of vegetable dyes.*

A Touch of Europe

Rayon/Wool/Silk, Wool/Silk, Silk & Cotton

Some of interior designer **Linda Abernathy**'s happiest childhood memories are of touring her great-uncle's woolen mills in Quebec.

"I loved seeing how my favorite soft 'happy' colors found themselves woven alongside some of my least favorite 'rude' colors, and early on I came to view every room as a naked friend waiting to be dressed," recalls this romantic.

That early appreciation of color and fabrics later carried Abernathy into a decorating career with endless opportunities to dress rooms with

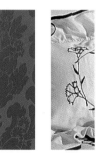

opulence, planned clutter and ravishing details, as shown in this 1920s town house that once belonged to Rita Hayworth.

ABOVE & RIGHT *The wall surrounding the faux marble fireplace is covered with a bright yet elegant cotton French toile that picks up the red of the Staffordshire and Wedgwood china. The toile is also used for the pull-down shades and to edge the antique silk damask-upholstered chairs. The exceedingly feminine look is given one masculine touch — a hefty ottoman covered with vintage striped silk.*

Photography by Anthony Peres

LEFT & ABOVE *A boxy room with little interest was transformed by hand-textured paint selected in a hue to complement the room's true focal point, an exuberant wool/silk floral tapestry used for chairs, tablecloth and an unusual swing-arm window treatment. A hand-painted border of cherubs and garlands further carries out the tapestry's rose-colored bouquets.*

ABOVE & LEFT *To visually expand a small master bedroom, rustic greenhouse doors were mounted above the bed and mirrored, integrating the space with the charming terrace beyond. Handpainted on the wall between the doors is the floral design of the cheerful ribbon-and-floral chintz used for balloon valances and shades. Hand-embroidered Egyptian blue-and-white cotton, which the designer found on one of her annual buying trips abroad, is used for bedspread, dust ruffle and shams.*

LEFT *Linda Abernathy select-ed this rayon/wool/silk tapestry with a vine motif to make a tiny powder room reminiscent of the owner's terraced Italian villa. The wallcovering pattern is installed upside down to make the vine appear as if it is growing from the roof.*

ABOVE *Blue-and-white country French cotton toile opens up this master bedroom, which in fact needed to be protected from its busy street location. Heavy padding on the walls provides an additional sound barrier. Cotton pull-down laminated shades allow sunlight to filter in while protecting the room's privacy. The quilted box valances repeat the twin quilted bedspread borders.*

Gothic Finery

Silk

No wonder this southern designer specializes in draping windows. **Mary Tait**'s touch is so graceful and her approach always so sensitively wedded to the particular situation that no one will let her do anything else.

For the living room in the New Orleans residence of Jim Reid Holden, who is known for entertaining with elegance, her decision was to dress the windows with the same level of finery that his frequent guests enjoy. For all curtains and shades she selected Venetian silk velvet for its subtle iridescence and lush body, and then proceeded to apply a Gothic stencil design with gold and silver paints, their metallic luster complementing the antiquity of the overall style and the rich materials found in the home's other furnishings.

"In all cases, one must use the fabric most appropriate for the function of the curtains and the purpose of the room in terms of the individuals living there," she says. "In this case, with formal entertainment being so much a part of the client's lifestyle, the room demanded a most luxurious and unusual texture at the windows — one that would also absorb and soften sound as well as ensure that, although the room was to be a formal gathering place, it would have hospitable warmth."

ALL *A twelve-inch-wide Gothic design was stenciled along leading edges and across the base of the room's Venetian silk velvet curtains and shades. The accompanying finials on the iron rods were fashioned as Gothic crosses in relief.*

Photography by Tina Freeman

A Cultivated Grace

Cotton, Polyester, Silk, Linen, Cotton Linen, Leather & Wool

The glorious location and style of the newly built residence of Curt and Gerry Pindler, on the Sherwood Valley Country Club in Thousand Oaks, California, make it feel like a villa on the Mediterranean. Yet the challenge of new homes, no matter how traditional their profile, is the hard-edged freshness of their finishes, which countered the sense of an estab-

lished history of gracious living that their owners wished to express. Enter interior designer *Valerie Bernard-Eglit*.

"The residence started as an empty shell with white walls and some shortcomings which were unable to be changed architecturally," she says. "So I replaced the moldings with ones of more substance, treated them and the walls as well as fireplaces and cabinets with a faux finish for a look of age, and, since Mr. Pindler is president of a major wholesale fabric house, used fabrics as lavishly as I wished. For example, I was able to overcome problematic window placements by a variety of drapery treatments and window dressings."

Such use of fabrics, plus a plethora of antiques and reproductions, enabled Bernard-Eglit to create the look of such a gracefully classical villa that the Pindlers' new home soon conveyed an air of having evolved over a long period of gracious living and privileged collecting.

LEFT *Shirred chamois-colored silk dresses both walls and vanity in the powder room. The black of the vanity's granite top is echoed by the handpainted classical wreath on its face which has been faux-finished, the black gesso figures on the key of the antique gold mirror, and the white oak floor's inlaid feature strip.*

BELOW *Framing the garden doors and serving as a backdrop to the dining table is bronze silk draped from a curtain rod with a tortoise shell faux finish and gold rose-and-acanthus leaf centerpiece. The Fortuny-style light fixture is a pale cream-colored silk painted with gold and bronze.*

Photography by Tim Street-Porter

LEFT *Softly draped hand-painted silk softens the top and post of a French four-poster iron bed from Ken Hansen, while an arched drapery treatment, smocked at the top and tied with tassels, creates an interesting frame for the French doors.*

ABOVE *In the master bedroom, an oak-hued polished cotton brings the look of Fortuny to the lavishly draped bed and windows. The window draperies are hung from an eighteenth-century French curtain rod. The Painted Room created a trompe l'oeil motif around the windows and door, and, above the door, a trompe l'oeil oeil-de-boeuf window.*

Relaxed Formality

Mohair, Silk, Cotton, Leather, Wool & Silk/Cotton

Today, even if one's fortunes were to include an elegant period home with enormous rooms, the inclination would likely be to not live with all the pomp and hired help its style would suggest. If money would not prohibit it, a preference for informal living most certainly would.

Given that logic, **Sandra Nunnerley** designed this room at the Kips Bay Boys' and Girls' Club Designer Showhouse as a multi-

functional room which could serve as living room, library and dining room. To do so, she swapped yester-year's penchant for huge sit-down feasts for a pared-down version at a round table that a party of two or eight could find equally elegant but more cozily hospitable. Yet when larger groups do gather, the long refectory table, usually used as a desk, serves as a buffet.

The room's multifunctional aspect also went a long way toward meeting the challenge of creating an intimate feeling within such a cavernous space that is also windowless. In addition, Nunnerley designed an exceptionally tall banquette to more protectively ensconce diners, installed large moldings to visually lower the room's potentially impersonal height, and designed four bookcases reminiscent of old library stairs to visually contain the room's distant corners. Finally, most important, she dressed the room with an array of fabrics that are so inventively draped, hung, trimmed and juxtaposed that one could need no view other than gazing at them.

LEFT *The exaggerated height of the banquette provides a grand canvas for the cotton brocades. The pillows are covered with two different fabrics as well, a solid silk taffeta on one side and a striped silk moiré on the other, providing an easy way for the host or hostess to create a change of pace.*

Photography by Feliciano

OPPOSITE *A heavy brushed cotton stripe punctuates a cigarette table, while silk pillows against mohair make the sofa the most luxurious seat in the house.*

Photography by Michael Mundy

ABOVE *Unlined silk taffeta in slate blue and cream makes the most of the door in this windowless room.*

Photography by Michael Mundy

Gossamer Dreams

Silk, Cotton & Nylon

To design a young lady's bedroom that would spell romance in a way that would feel more like the 1990s than the 1890s, **Susan Federman** used a wealth of gloriously sensuous fabrics but kept the feeling light and airy through whisper-fresh colors and graceful draping techniques.

A lilting array of silks she had custom-dyed and hand-painted an inviting combination of cream, rose, taupe and browny peach with a touch of pale green. These she combined with cotton moiré on a lounge chair, silk organza at the windows and, on a bench, crushed velvet tied with velvet rose petals. The bed itself, made from an eighteenth-century Italian valance with carved side rails gilded to match, is draped with an enchantment of cream, green and wheat-hued silk that seems nothing less than a ballgown.

ABOVE & RIGHT *Hushed hues of airy fabrics and delicately crafted Italian and French eighteenth-century furniture turn a bedroom into a living daydream. To give the painted walls as much depth and luminescence as the silk they surround, Lynne Rutter Decorative Painting added stripes of pearl and taupe glaze that were then hand-rubbed to soften their edges and topped with a light white glaze.*

Photography by David Livingston

OPPOSITE & ABOVE *Blue denim rises to new heights in this master bedroom suite.*

Natural Imprints

Dialogue With Nature

Cotton, Linen, Linen/Cotton & Wool

In the design of Villa Belvedere, **Giancarlo Alhadeff**'s intention was to meet the clients' desire to live in a house bathed in light and visibly wrapped with their breathtaking site — high up in the tree-laden Bergamo Hills and looking north toward the Alps. In response to this and other requests, the Milanese architect created a rigorous

design in which a few well-chosen materials, including fabrics limited in number but highly important in their functional and aesthetic use, play a major part in creating a dialogue with the mountain panorama.

For example, the exterior entry is characterized by river stones, and the interior flooring of Palladian terrazzo (*seminato alla veneziana*) buoys every area with a subtly pinkish sheen. "I have a distinct preference for natural colors in interiors and I am fascinated by the use of warm palette stones, because, while they are warm in color, they are cool to the touch," says Alhadeff. "Yet, because they are basically neutral, they also allow for greater possibilities in the treatment of windows and furniture."

Working with interior designer **Piero Pinto**, Alhadeff decided to continue the tranquilly neutral palette in most of the upholstered furniture and window treatments to further amplify the home's spacious feeling and give full play to its splendid setting.

LEFT *Untreated cotton on the "Nonnamaria" lounge chairs and ottomans from Flexform strikes a contemporary note atop a nineteenth-century Persian carpet.*

BELOW *In the master bathroom, an automatic skylight closure incorporates undyed natural cotton. The fabric panels at the windows are of linen. The "Karina" chair was designed by Mancini and Dorell for Sawaya & Moroni.*

OPPOSITE *English floral fabric brings a colorful garden effect to the conservatory off the living room. The same fabric is used to upholster the nineteenth-century Italian settee. "Dick Deck" beechwood chairs by Philippe Starck for Aleph's Ubik Collection add another jolt of color.*

Photography by Studio Acqua

Weekend Habit

Linen, Linen/Cotton, Silk, Wool & Cotton

Sherri Donghia is so drawn to fabrics that, when she isn't designing them, she's collecting them. Her passion for textiles permeates her Long Island weekend home with a highly spirited yet totally relaxed look.

A timberwork house customized by **Donghia**'s husband, **Roger Eulau**, and architect **Richard Lear** provides a welcome respite from her

weekdays in New York. The home's airiness and natural hues for walls and floors create an ideal background for the textiles she has acquired from her trips throughout the world developing business and new designs for Donghia, the interior furnishings firm founded by her cousin Angelo Donghia.

The way she hangs, drapes and upholsters with these acquisitions is fascinating. Scarves she found in Indonesia have become wall hangings. Ceremonial cloths she sighted in Sweden are now used as throws. Indian rugs for which she bartered in Santa Fe have been turned into pillows.

The one thing this devoted collector will not do is put her treasured fabrics away. Says Donghia, "Beautiful fabrics should never be stored in the closet. They are meant to be seen and touched!"

ABOVE *The original South American hand-woven cotton hammocks which inspired the Donghia Hamaca Collection today inspire lazy afternoons at Sherri Donghia's weekend home.*

RIGHT *Donghia's "Kent Camelback" sofa dressed with Donghia's "Relaxed Linen" slipcover is accented with pillows covered with tone-on-tone crewelwork of wool embroidered on a cotton ground and antique American Indian striped cloth of silk and wool.*

Photography by Scott Frances/Esto

OPPOSITE *An Indonesian cotton ikat used as a throw is paired with colorful Indian crewel pillows of wool embroidered on a cotton ground. The bedcover is hand-loomed linen and wool.*

ABOVE *Donghia's "Saratoga" sofa upholstered in "Hamaca Rojo" handwoven cotton continues inside the colorful South American accent of the hammock (page 128) which inspired the fabric collection.*

RIGHT *Linen/cotton-blend damask and an antique American Indian silk and wool stripe fabric enhance the pillows on a club sofa with linen slipcover.*

Rancho Diablo

Cotton, Wool & Leather

When Ace Architects' **David Weingarten** acquired this 1930s hunting lodge in the hills east of San Francisco, he and his partner **Lucia Howard** aimed to make it more an expression of early California than it had ever been before.

Built by architect Lilian B. Bridgman for Dr. Clarence Wills,

father of Olympic and Wimbledon tennis star Helen Wills Moody, the home's two-thousand-square-foot space had fallen into unimaginable disrepair and had been subjected to various unsightly additions. Yet, by the time these were removed and the original handpainted tile, hand-forged hardware and whitewashed brick retained and repaired, a remarkable transformation had occurred. The retreat's former Wild West character had been not only reestablished, but also, by the addition of a furnishings mix the designers call "Exuberant Ranch Style," infused with a new spirit completely its own.

LEFT *An extensive cactus garden serves as preamble to the highly romantic hunting lodge with its redwood board-and-batten siding, unfinished brick and handmade roof tiles.*

BOTTOM LEFT *A bedspread made of printed cotton combines with a Navajo rug in colorful profusion. Beside the fireplace are two Spanish Gothic chairs upholstered in embroidered cotton prints.*

ABOVE *Under the original structure's protectively oversized redwood beams, the interior mingles antique Navajo rugs and a '30s-era Monterey furniture collection with contemporary cowhide chairs.*

OPPOSITE *Leather curtains in "Rancho Diablo" red and black, held on wrought-iron rods, are made in bold geometric patterns to echo the color and feeling of Weingarten's collection of Navajo rugs.*

Photography by Alan Weintraub

Wine Country Native

Silk/Linen, Silk & Cotton

The California wine country inspires some to go native and others, who already are earth spirits, to move there. Long before she and her husband migrated to Sonoma, textile designer and manufacturer **Barbara Beckmann** was promoting and using an ecologically balanced system of

fabric and dye stuffs. Her affinity to nature made this particular valley, with its rustic, unblemished setting, seem ideal for one who had vowed to "not use dyes that are toxic to the environment or to us."

So Beckmann asked architect **Robert G. Zinkhan, Jr.** and contractor Gary Burlington to extend a contemporary ranch-style home she found there. After Beckmann herself designed the interiors as so many comforting oases of fabric, she knew she truly had "come home." Indeed, she named a new collection of cottons and linens that she designed specifically for this house after the neighboring wine-country town of Santa Rosa.

LEFT *Individually covered cushions on stairs leading to the study provide inviting resting spots for gatherings large and small.*

RIGHT *The visual poetry of white-on-white, created by white silk leaves on white pepper silk, makes the wicker lounge chair seem literally ensconced beneath the oak beyond.*

Photography by Douglas Sandberg

ABOVE *Three of Beckmann's hand-printed fabrics, combined into a one-of-a-kind wall hanging on silk, create an ideal portal through which to pass to the real garden beyond. It is from creating such pieces that she develops her ideas for future fabric collections.*

RIGHT *To Babara Beckmann, her garden provides the best light for seeing color and the best atmosphere for dreaming of new ones. Those shown here were all inspired by the hues surrounding them.*

FAR RIGHT *When not being worn, Barbara Beckmann Designs' wearable art becomes an art object for the home.*

Barefoot and Happy

Linen/Cotton, Cotton & Sea Grass

"I want to avoid monotony and create wonderful sensations," says **Sig Bergamin**. To this Brazilian designer headquartered in New York, there's no rule that can't be broken, and, especially in a too-uptight and pressure-packed world, no comfort that should be overlooked. So his major goal in these two showcase houses was simply to provide relaxed and cozy spaces — plus a welcome dose of his exotic South American spirit!

ABOVE *"I have no fear of mixing prints, textures and colors," says Bergamin of this dining room. Its exotic punch comes from a patchwork of thirty-two different floral cotton and linen fabrics that he cut, stripped and arranged on the spot.*

LEFT & RIGHT *Under the eaves of a large, rambling, summer cottage in Southampton, Long Island, Bergamin created a bedroom as foot-loose-and-fancy-free as any beachside cabana could possibly be. Floral cotton prints join the designer's own Indian textile, 1940s area rug and a carpet of sea grass.*

Photography by John Hall

Cape Cod Lightly

Cotton/Linen, Linen, Cotton, Cotton/Rayon, Polyester, Wool, Raffia & Leather

Mostly natural hues in richly textured weaves with an assortment of stripes and subtle patterns kept surfacing on **Gari Sprott** and **John Nichols**'s worktable during the design development of Deep Water, this home on the

ruggedly beautiful Cape Cod shore. Their rather traditionally minded clients wanted this particular residence to be a bit less serious and lighter in feeling than their others are, yet the predictable nautical direction that many would have deemed the answer did not tempt Sprott and Nichols in the slightest. Instead, they listened to the soft gray blue of the sea, sky, winter woods and the

LEFT *The partially existing "modern Cape Cod" structure was enlarged with sensitivity to the local architecture and stained with Cabot's "Pewter Grey," a color typical to salt-air weathered shingles.*

BELOW *In the living room, subtle patterns and hues reflect without competing with the soft Cape Cod naturescape beyond.*

Cape architecture, which they completely refinished and partially rebuilt, and allowed the interior palette to evolve over time.

In the end, the recurring grid that now does show up on balcony railings, windows, furniture and fabrics is so pervasive that one might think it had been predetermined, as if it were a designer's idea of what a Cape Cod home should be regardless of the way it actually is. One might think that — except for the way it fits so appropriately this particular location and interprets so precisely its owners request.

"We felt very good that this grid leitmotif truly did emanate *from* the unique situation rather than being superimposed *on* it," says Sprott.

ABOVE *A hand-loomed cotton flat-weave rug underscores the grid that recurs throughout the design, echoing the buttoned-up attitude of the architecture and the slightly structured feeling of old Cape Cod.*

Photography by Peter Vitale

RIGHT *In the master bedroom, the revered Cape Cod is both reality and, in Thomas B. Higham's* Clouds over Crosby's at the Turn of the Tide, *art. Save for a dreamland of greige and cream, what else could one need?*

Beachfront Serenity

Polyester, Cotton, Silk, Silk/Cotton, Wool/Rayon & Leather

It is amazing how often a second home looks just like its owners' main residence, denying the chance for a change of pace. Not so this penthouse in Palm Beach, Florida, completely renovated by **Victoria Hagan**.

The serenity one has come to expect in all interiors designed by Hagan is doubled here, where colors, details, and the type and amount of furnishings all contribute to its being as much a sea of calm as the ocean beyond on the most placid day possible.

"My clients wanted the interior to relate to the setting while not competing with their art collection, and I myself like to bring the outside in," says Hagan. "Since this particular setting was on the water, all fabrics and colors needed to subtly refer to the sand, water and sky."

Indeed. The sheers are as translucent as ocean spray, the silk curtains like a breeze keeping time with the surf, the luxurious leathers as pliable as sand, and the hushed hues as ethereal as light.

The softly sculpted lines of the pared-down design remind one of sand dunes and gently rolling waves. Even the carpet was custom-woven wall-to-wall so that no seam might interrupt the hushed, sandy-greige expanse.

"I wanted it to be a relaxed and easy space," Hagan comments. "Isn't that what a good interior is all about?"

LEFT *Sheer curtains add softness while not blocking the light.*

Photography by Steven Brooke

BELOW *A leather chair and ottoman add a softly sculptured quality to the living room.*

OPPOSITE *In the master bedroom, breezily light silk and painted glass mimic the ocean's celadon hues, while the oil painting by Milton Avery echoes the sea in the study beyond.*

Reincarnations

Cotton, Wool & Silk

Somehow it is possible to retain feelings for the past as well as push onward. In these two rooms, *Mark Zeff* juggles both feelings at once.

In one, a dining room created when deconstruction was the rage, he was inspired by a house he had seen in Vicenza, Italy, a palace with

decaying rooms. The traditional method of placing fabric on the walls allowed the fabric to provide a base which was then further decorated. In this dining room, Zeff's goal was to expose this practice. "One could say the deconstructivist treatment of the Fortuny silk serves both symbolic and functional purposes," Zeff notes. "One can see it as symbolizing the past as seen from today's perspective and also as setting the right analytical note for stimulating dinner converations."

In the other room, a dressing area off a master bedroom where he wanted to establish a sense of relaxed restfulness for study and contemplation, Zeff tented the walls with a heavy, natural Haitian cotton. What formerly were dark paneled walls now feel like a blank canvas, ready to receive inspired thought without interruption.

"I usually drape a room when its condition is so bad that painting won't work," says Zeff. "But in this situation, the draped walls symbolize, as well as hopefully help carry forth, the room's meditative purpose."

ABOVE *Printed silk was applied to the wall, then partially removed to expose the artifice of covering, i.e., hiding the truth, with fabric. The silk's being printed to look like tapestry provides another aspect of artificiality to be examined.*

RIGHT *Natural fabrics in neutral or bleached tones create a blank canvas for a room meant for study and meditation.*

Photography courtesy of Mark Zeff Consulting Group, Inc.

A Delicate Peace

Cotton, Silk, Rayon, Cotton/Rayon, Cotton/Polyester, Wool, Linen & Metallics

"Fabrics should be used as points of encounter rather than as a general theme. They should stimulate, but not cause visual fatigue," says designer/contractor *Joan Moseley*, who has restored and remodeled numerous

Craftsman houses in Southern California. Her dedicated involvement with such regional landmarks as homes by Greene and Greene, Roland Coates, Reginald Johnson and Wallace Neff has led to her being a devotee of the quiet calm they exude and wanting to enhance but not disturb their delicately composed peace by the appropriate use of textiles.

Moseley had a chance to demonstrate her approach to fabrics anew when the contemporary studio adjacent to her 1907 Craftsman home was heavily damaged in the 1994 Northridge earthquake. By remaking her studio into a refuge of earthy wood, tile and stone inspired by her main house, she used fabrics exactly as she likes to use them — as colorful, comfortable and highly personal punctuations that celebrate life, yet without overriding the treasured tranquility of her favorite type of architecture.

OPPOSITE *Sometimes the fabric dictates its application, as in the case of Barbara Beckmann's "Pesche," which became a door hanging instead of a scarf treatment so that it could be seen flat rather than gathered or draped.*

Photography by Anthony Peres

BELOW *Fabric samples combine with a glorious assortment of fabrics used for pillows and throws, a celebratory door treatment and even a cover for the copy machine.*

LEFT *Joan Moseley juxtaposes personality as well as color with the quiet woods and Craftsman-style furniture of her studio.*

RIGHT *The spa, left relatively undamaged by the earthquake and now restored, is complemented by granite to tie in with the Batchelder-like field tiles no longer in production, as well as oases of fabric.*

LEFT & ABOVE *A galaxy of pillows and throws, each richly textured fabric finished with one of the many trims that delight Joan Moseley, makes the loft a welcoming respite from the custom worktable below (fabricated by William Stranger). "Since there are firms today doing custom trims with as little as a five-yard minimum, one is free to tie the most unrelated fabrics into a congruent whole," she says.*

Spinning Yarns

Polyester, Acetate, Rayon, Viscose/Cotton, Silk & Bamboo

Comfort, scale, harmony and the relationship of textures, colors and materials — these all are reflected in "A Room of One's Own" designed by **Clodagh** for the Kips Bay Boys & Girls Club Decorator Showhouse.

A collage of the designer's own memories, experiences, travels and sensations, it is an exciting as well as cozily comfortable place to gather before the fireside either with guests or for quiet contemplation. Its

furnishings, all of which she designed, represent the primitive references to earth that have always inspired her.

As Clodagh herself says, "The room, like life, is layered. It is full of loved books, maquettes, materials and texture, and perfumed with the warm, fresh fragrance of rosemary and gorse."

Nostalgia that appeals to all the senses was again given expression in the kitchen Clodagh designed with architect Robert Pierpont for Stone House. The smooth coolness of satiny plaster, the texture of recycled brick, sensually heavy silk and velvet around a generously massive dining table — all evoke feelings of comforting familiarity that one loves to touch as well as see.

LEFT *Sensual, handpainted rayon velvet in soft amber covers armchair and ottoman. The digital collage, a photographic "Biograph" of Clodagh's life by Daniel Aubry, incorporates a wealth of memorabilia.*

BELOW *Tall-backed chairs are upholstered with dramatically handpainted cotton velour. Bamboo shades veil the window, and handpainted sheers hang from a patinated copper rod. Over the sheers are layered, handpainted curtains that add depth and luster to the overall scheme.*

LEFT *The earthily hued fabrics are enhanced by the glow of two vast elliptical lighting fixtures designed by Clodagh and placed on either side of the fireplace. The mechanical fixture at the ceiling, as well as the floor lamp, were made by Daniel Berglund from salvaged car parts.*

Photography by Daniel Aubry

ABOVE & RIGHT *At Stone House, an array of fabrics in earthy Roman reds, warm ambers and rich golds serves as foil for stenciled designs, including various mottoes the home's owners helped gather.*

FAR RIGHT *The furnishings in this Kips Bay Showhouse room, all designed by Clodagh, include a luxurious sofa-daybed on wheels upholstered with amber-colored viscose/cotton chenille and a screen inspired by Masai shields.*

Getaway Modes

Polyester & Spandex

It is no coincidence that the luminous, fluid fabric structures by **Gisela Stromeyer** seem to dance through space. Before studying architecture in Munich and finishing at Pratt Institute in New York, this fourth-generation member of a family of famous German tentmakers was a dancer and has never ceased experiencing space through movement.

"To a dancer, space is fluid and the beauty of that fluidity is waiting to be defined through tension and relaxation, through flex and reflex," she says.

Light is also vital, she emphasizes, "Just as on stage, without light nothing happens."

Stromeyer first makes models of her stretched fabric creations, then cuts the fabric and supervises its installation. In every case her intention is to bring a feeling of weightlessness to a world too bound by gravity, and through her extraordinary ability to balance tension and tranquility, she gives the world yet another avenue by which to enrich and uplift our homes with fabric.

ABOVE & RIGHT *For a residence in Munich that has high ceilings and awkward proportions, spandex structures soften the lines and create a sense of intimacy without diminishing the rooms' soaring feeling. Lighting, as integral to the design as the fabric, turns each bedroom into a play of shadows at night.*

Photography by Thomas Mayfield

ABOVE *For the long, narrow entry to a meditation room designed by Clodagh, Gisela Stromeyer's translucent polyester sculpture twists and turns toward the central point where it opens toward the light. The acetate polyester fabric, which has been stretched into shape and then attached to the walls with small bronze hooks, is dyed amber.*

Photography by Michael Moran

ALL *Gisela Stromeyer's span-dex sculptures turn a loft residence into a translucent, airy cave. The fabric as well as the walls has been painted with cave painting motifs by artists* **Marianne van Lent** *and* **Karen Foote**.

Photography by
Michael Moran

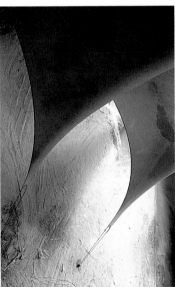

RESOURCES

PART I: Multicultural attire

COSMOPOLITAN PASTICHE

Pages 14-15 Wool (rugs, carpets, floor mat, needlepoint and tapestry): Christine Van der Hurd • Cotton (sofa upholstery, living room): Covington • Black-and-white cotton (chair upholstery, living room): Timney Fowler Ltd. • Silk brocade (living room valance and tie-backs): Royale • Cotton (headboard upholstery, bedroom): Timney Fowler Ltd. • White cotton matelassé (bedcovering): Anichini.

GLOBAL ENSEMBLE

Pages 16-19 Egyptian cotton damask (wallcovering): "Canterbury" from Jack Lenor Larsen • Silk (sofa): "Willow" from Jack Lenor Larsen • Jacquard worsted wool (seating, armchairs): Jack Lenor Larsen • Leather (sides and backs, armchairs): Larsen Leather • Silk (cushion, game table): "Shan" from Jack Lenor Larsen • Coir (carpet): "Chevron" from Larsen Carpet • Woven wicker (Larsen Loom dining chairs): Larsen Furniture • Jacquard cotton (sliding panels): "Brighton" from Jack Lenor Larsen • Machine-embroidered cotton over Mylar (bedspread): "Magnum" from Jack Lenor Larsen • Woven Egyptian cotton (casement): "Jason" from Jack Lenor Larsen • Woven leather (panels): "Wholly Cow" from Larsen Leather • Coir (floorcovering): Larsen Carpet • Nylon polyester (bronze bolster): "Cybelle" from Jack Lenor Larsen • Wool/cotton (pillow): designed by Junichi Arai.

RADIANT RAIMENT

Pages 20-23 Silk taffeta (drapery): "Du Barry Taffeta Stripe" from Christopher Norman, Inc. • Window treatments: Stables, Schwab & Trujillo, Inc. • Silk taffeta (barrel armchair): Nobilis Fontan, Inc. • Striped silk (pillows and armchairs): Nobilis Fontan, Inc. • Silk (sofa and banquette): Christopher Norman, Inc. • Viscose (trims): Houlès et Cie. • Upholstery fabrication (sofa and banquette): Juan Munoz • Upholstery fabrication (chairs): Abbots Co. Inc. • Silk/cotton (chair seats): "Satin Chine Chartreuse" from Clarence House • Silk Bemberg (tablecloth): "Vega Cornaline" from Clarence House • Cotton/linen (drapery): "Cinnebar Flame Spot" from Ken Bragaline, Inc. • Cotton ottoman (drapery and pillows): "Michelle ecru/noir" from Manuel Canovas, Inc. • Cotton (sofa): Diamond Foam & Fabric • Silk velvet (sofa trim): "Tiger Velvet" from Brunschwig & Fils, Inc. • Upholstery (sofa): Abbots Co., Inc.

AN ARTFUL RESPONSE

Pages 24-27 Cotton/rayon tapestry (throw pillows): "Tabriz" from Donghia Furniture/Textiles • Leather (sofa and chair): Spinneybeck • Cotton/acrylic tapestry (upholstered chair): "Sherlock Holmes" from Clarence House • Sisal (floorcovering): Signature Collection, custom, from Design Spec • Cotton/viscose chenille (drapery): custom from Van Vechten Textiles, Inc. through The Bradbury Collection • Cotton/polyester tapestry (end chairs): "Westminster Tapestry" from Yves Gonnet through Donghia Furniture/Textiles • Cotton chenille (side chairs): Clarence House.

FAR EASTERN CALM

Pages 28-31 All Asian antique furniture, textiles, accessories, lighting, blinds and floorcoverings through Charles Jacobsen, Inc. • Linen (upholstery): "Relaxed Linen" from Donghia Furniture/Textiles • Leather chaise: The Knoll Group • Linen (cushions): "Relaxed Linen" from Donghia Furniture/Textiles • Chinese sea grass (carpeting): S & J Biren, Inc. • Belgian linen (bed covering): Donghia Furniture/Textiles • Rayon/cotton-blend chenille (daybeds): "Portofino Double Weight," from Van Vechten Textiles & Furniture Inc. through The Bradbury Collection • Silk damask (bolsters): "Guinevere" from J. Robert Scott Textiles, Inc. • Silk (torchières): The Isamu Noguchi Foundation/Akari Associates.

INTERNATIONAL EVOLUTION

Pages 32-33 Fabrics (pillows): Indian shawl from a market in Jaipur, India; carpet remnants, flea market, Vienna; kimono sleeves, Japan; kimono cords (over Thai silk), from Ikeda Antique Textiles; various designer fabrics through Markasia • Linen (canopy): Western Market • Printed indigo cotton (*futon*): Blue and White • Hand-blocked printed silk (*kimono*): Ikeda Antique Textiles • Cotton ikat (*yukata* fabric covering tatami platform and tea chests): Ikeda Antique Textiles • Cotton, starch resist-painted with handpainted details (banner): Oriental Bazaar • Cotton canvas (lounge chairs): Luxhome • Printed cotton (door backing and bedspread piping): "Allison Floral" from Ralph Lauren Home Collection.

WORLDLY EXPRESSIONS

Pages 34-39 Silk (drapery, sheers and yellow-and-green upholstery): Scalamandré • Wool (needlepoint and flamestitch): Brunschwig & Fils Inc. • Silk (trim): Houlés-U.S.A. and Clarence House • Cottons (upholstery and drapery): Brunschwig & Fils Inc. • Cotton Twill (upholstery): Clarence House • Raw silk (upholstery): Old World Weavers • Silk velvet (leopard print): Clarence House • Cashmere (print): Grey Watkins Ltd. • Leather: custom-dyed, Spinneybeck Enterprises Inc. • Wool (flamestitch): Brunschwig & Fils Inc. • Combed cotton (Corn Yellow upholstery): Lee Jpfa, Inc. • Mohair (ikat): Clarence House • Silk (plaid): Brunschwig & Fils Inc. • Silk ikat (bed drapery): "Chemer" from Brunschwig & Fils Inc. • Wool (flamestitch): Brunschwig &Fils Inc. • Combed cotton (corn yellow upholstery): Lee Jofa, Inc. • Six-ply silk (bed treatment's inner lining, chairs and bench): custom color from Fonthill Ltd.

HERMÈS FASHION SHOW

Pages 40-41 Silk (backs of fauteuils, front of desk chair and pillows): Hermès of Paris • Raffia (fronts of fauteuils): Donghia Furnitures/Textiles • Saddle leather (side chair and back of desk chair): Hermès of Paris • Wool (horse blankets): Hermès of Paris • Mink (throw cover): Hermès of Paris • Cotton (sofa and Mike Moore's "Jean-Michel" lounge chair): Henry Calvin Fabrics • Cotton (Mike Moore's "Fabulous Club Chairs"): "Sienna" from Donghia Furniture/Textiles • Sisal (floorcovering): Alison T. Seymour, Inc. through Abbey Carpets.

ENGLISH COTTAGE SNUGGERY

Pages 42-43 Cotton/rayon needlepoint tapestry (loveseat): Clarence House • Silk and linen (pillows): recut and redesigned from various sources • Indian cotton (drapery): Fonthill Ltd. • Hand-tied silk fringe (drapery trim): Manuel Canovas • Silk and wool needlepoint tapestry (rug): antique, client's collection • Linen (wing chair): Carleton V, Ltd. • Cotton chintz (drapery and bed coverlet): "Ariana" from Brunschwig & Fils, Inc. • Silk fabrics and braids (pillows): vintage • Silks and silk velvets (headboard): Brunschwig & Fils, Inc. • Rayon taffeta (dust ruffle): Sahco Hesslein Collection through Bergamo Fabrics Inc.

SHALL WE DANCE?

Pages 44-45 Unglazed cotton (wallcovering): Colefax and Fowler • Glazed cotton solids (canopy lining and pillows): Colefax and Fowler • Glazed cotton prints (outer canopy and table skirts): Laura Ashley, Inc. • Wool (carpet): Trade France • Fabrics workshop: Trade France.

EVENING DRESS

Pages 46-47 Bleached sisal (carpet): The Natural Floorcovering Centre • Wool (area rug): Caucasian kilim from Nazar Rug Galleries • Viscose modacrylic (ottoman): "Khiva" from Osborne & Little, fabricated by Aaron Upholstery • Viscose modacrylic (slipper chair): "Pichola" from Osborne & Little, fabricated by Aaron Upholstery • Cotton damask (sofa): "Cosca Damask" from Stroheim & Romann • Hand-printed silk (roman blinds): "Animal Medallion" through Chawton House • Hand-printed silk (curtains): "Classical Stars" from Celia Birtwell through Chawton House • Silk (curtains): Sericus Silks • Silk (cushions and trim): Jagtar Silks and G.P. & J.Baker through St. James Furnishings.

FRENCH LIBERTIES

Pages 48-49 Aubusson rug: Vojtech Blau, Inc. • Silk brocades (drapery and canapés), silk velour (chairs) and trimmings: Scalamandré • Viscose/linen/cotton moiré (banquettes): Old World Weavers, Inc. • Leather (game chairs): Clarence House • Matte silk faille (walls): Scalamandré • Watered-silk taffeta (overcurtains): Brunschwig & Fils Inc. • Silk satin (chairs): Cowtan & Tout • Pongee silk (sheers): Jack Lenor Larsen Inc. • Wool (carpet): Patterson, Flynn, Martin & Manges, Inc. • Cotton block print (bed): Brunschwig & Fils Inc. • Linen (walls): Clarence House • Cotton *millefleurs* print (windows): Cowtan & Tout • Thai silk (chair): Jack Lenor Larsen.

PART II: City Suiting

DELIGHT TO HAND AND EYE

Pages 52-55 Silk taffeta (drapery, sofa and chairs): Scalamandré • Silk brocade (throw pillows): made from four antique fabric panels, through Rose Cumming Chintzes, Ltd. • Wool tapestry (ottomans): early-nineteenth-century French tapestry, designer's collection • Sisal (floorcovering throughout): Patterson, Flynn, Martin & Manges • Leather (chairs): Libra Leather, Inc. • Silk woven with threads of gold (sari cloth used as tablecloth): from Northern India through Marjorie Reed Gordon • Linen

cotton (drapery, headboard, dust skirt and chair): Hinson & Company • Cotton sheers (drapery): Hinson & Company • White wool (throw) and black cotton matelassé (coverlet): E. Braun & Co., Inc. • White cotton linens bordered with black cotton and linen (sheets): Anichini • Silk (bed treatment and window drapery): "Morning Star" from Jack Lenor Larsen • Wool (bench fabric): J. Robert Scott Textiles, Inc. • Silk crepe de Chine (blanket cover and European sham): E. Braun & Co., Inc. • Cotton striae (gold gilt chair): Henry Calvin Fabrics • Camel's hair (throw): E. Braun & Co., Inc. • Wool tapestry (pillows on bench): antique tapestry through Kentshire Galleries.

PLANES IN SPACE

Pages 56-57 Stainless steel mesh (panels): Gretchen Bellinger Inc. • Panel fabrication: Woodwork Corporation of America • Wool (sofa): Interior Crafts Inc. • Leather (Barcelona chairs): Barksdale Rudd Inc. • Wool (sofa, foreground): Jack Lenor Larsen • Racing car wool, dark green (two-seater sofa): Scalamandré • Silk (throw pillows): Jim Thompson Thai Silk/through Holly Hunt Ltd. • Silk (drapery): Gretchen Bellinger Inc. • Leather (Barcelona chairs and stools): Interior Crafts.

INDOOR HEAVEN

Pages 58-59 Cotton/rayon gold lamé (ceiling): "All That Glitters" from Gretchen Bellinger Inc. • Rayon sheer (ceiling): Schumacher • Mohair (living room chairs): DesignTex Fabrics Inc. • Wool rug (living room): Carousel Carpet Mills Inc. • Black leather (chairs, living room): by Leon Jaloe, France, circa 1928 • Russian red leather (cab chair, at dining table): by Mario Bellini • Leather (settees, family room): Cascade Upholstery • Rug (family room): Carl T. Chew through Mia Gallery.

JAPANESE HOME, WESTERN DRESS

Pages 60-61 Silk (drapery): Samro Textiles, JAB Joseph Anstoetz through JAB Anstoetz Inc. • Cotton brocade (purple chairs): China Seas, Inc. through Habert & Associates • Silk and viscose (plaid chairs and pillows): Telio & Cie • Wool (carpet): Stark Carpet Corporation.

WELL-ORDERED CALM

Pages 62-63 Polyester: Ultrasuede HP® through American Décor • Leather (black sofa): from Novita Couros • Cotton (ivory colored chair): from Beraldin Tecidos Ltda • Cotton (yellow chair): Status, Tecidos Ltrda • Wool (carpet): designed by artist Paulo Segall, fabricated by Neva, Tapetes • Silk (sofa and curtains): Beraldin Tecidos Ltda • Cotton (armchair): handpainted by artist Marco Mariutti • Wool (carpet): designed by Arthur de Mattos Casas, fabricated by Neva, Tapetes • Cotton (armchair): Status, Tecidos LTDA • Wool (carpet): designed by artist Paulo Segall, fabricated by Neva, Tapetes.

POINT OF VIEW
Pages 64-67   Silk/polyester (drapery): Maharam • Cotton (sheers): Maharam • Cotton chenille (sofa): "Malibu" from California Pacific • Raw linen/silk (club chair): California Pacific • Cotton/silk moiré (small pillows with fringe): Calico Corners • Silk (large pillows with fringe): "Nanking Silk" from California Pacific.

LOFT-STYLE INGENUITY
Pages 68-69

CHIC, NOT SLEEK
Pages 70-71   Woven-leather textiles: E.N.T. incorporated.

EMBELLISHED MUSIC
Pages 72-73   Cotton (screen): "Pentagramma" by Gaston Y Daniela through St. James Furnishings • Cotton (tub chair): "Trevi" from Stroheim & Romann through Seneca • Thai silk, hand-woven, six-ply (sofa): Peuanthai • Silk (armchair): "Trellis" from Jagtar • Silk damask (ottoman): "Belvedere" from Jim Thompson through Arkitex • Cotton (bergere chairs): from Etamine La Maison, through South Pacific Fabrics • Silk (pillows): "Mantua Star" from Osborne & Little through Wardlaw Pty Ltd, "Palace Grille" and "Loggia Vine" from Jim Thompson through Arkitex, "Cupid" from Royalston House • Jute and raw silk (trimming): Passementeries • Upholstery fabrication: Aaron Upholstery • Pillow fabrication: BQ Designs • Wool (area rugs): antique Caucasian rugs, The Natural Floorcovering Centre.

SKY-HIGH EUPHORIA
Pages 74-75   Cotton ottoman (chairs): "Domicile" from Fuggerhaus through Christopher Hyland, Inc., handpainted by Carla Weisberg • Wool (Aubusson carpet): antique, Sotheby's • Silk taffeta (shades): Christopher Hyland, Inc. • Wool silk (carpet): V'Soske, custom-designed by Carla Weisberg • Silk (sofa and chairs): Jack Lenor Larsen • Leather (piping): Spinneybeck • Wool (carpet): Elizabeth Eakins, Inc., custom-designed by Emanuela Frattini Magnusson.

ELOQUENT LAYERING
Pages 76-77   Silk scrim and cotton blackout lining (drapery): Groundworks through Lee Jofa, Inc. • Leather (lounge chair and ottoman): Spinneybeck • Waxed, handpainted cotton (armchairs): designers' collection • Mohair (sofa): Maharam • Red leather (Donghia game chairs): Donghia Furniture/Textiles • Leather-banded granite cocktail table: Bonaventure Furniture Industries Ltd. • Mohair (sofa and ottomans): Donghia Furniture/Textiles • Rayon (lounge chair and footstool): International Fabrics, Inc. • Embossed rayon (window shades): Innovations in Wallcoverings • Leather (cornices and trim): Spinneybeck • Wool (carpet): Masland Carpets Inc. • Wool (area rug): Carpet Innovations, Inc. • Mohair (armchairs): Scalamandré • Linen chenille (chair): Henry Calvin Fabrics • Textured cotton (sofa): Manuel Canovas, Inc.

PIECES OF SKY
Pages 78-79   Canvas (paintings): Lammy Weisman • Linen (modular sofa): Bernhardt • Cotton (bedspread): "Quadrilateral" by Marimekko • Wool (chair and upholstery, bedroom): Cassina.

UTTER OPULENCE
Pages 80-81   Woven cotton (ceiling and walls): Stroheim & Romann, Inc. • Woven, nubby cotton (upholstered furniture): Henry Calvin Fabrics • Cotton/rayon chenille: Van Vechten Textiles, Inc. through The Bradbury Collection • Cotton/linen (bedhanging): Henry Calvin Fabrics through Keith H. McCoy & Associates • Cotton/linen wall upholstery: Pindler & Pindler, Inc. • Cotton piqué with silk grosgrain ribbon (bedspread): O'Shea Custom • Silk (bedhanging): Scalamandré • Cotton piqué (bedspread): O'Shea Custom • Silk (chair): Nancy Corzine • Cotton/linen (window treatment): Henry Calvin Fabrics through Keith McCoy & Associates.

FORMAL WEAR
Pages 82-85   Wool (rug): antique Persian from Mansour • Suede (Duo lounge chair, custom-designed by Richard Mayhew and Mark Enos): from Said Falati and Ron Gucciardo • Leather (Duo dining chair): Spinneybeck • Upholstery fabrication (Duo chairs, custom-designed by Richard Mayhew and Mark Enos): JJ Custom • Cotton (Duo chaise, custom-designed by Richard Mayhew and Mark Enos): Jack Lenor Larsen • Fabrication (Duo chaise): A. Rudin • Silk (drapery): "Celestial Cherub" from Jack Lenor Larsen • Cotton/rayon (drapery trimming): West Coast Trimming Corporation • Drapery fabrication: Raymond Gorini • Fabrication and installation (wallcovering): Rod Martin Company • Wool (rug): antique Oushak from Emser Carpets • Silk (drapery): "Celestial Gild" from Jack Lenor Larsen • Rayon (drapery tiebacks): Houlès-U.S.A. • Linen (bed drapery and chaise): "Laroche Oyster" from Donghia Furniture/Textiles • Drapery fabrication (bed and window): Raymond Gorini • Upholstery fabrication (chaise and slipcover): A. Rudin • Leather (desk chair): antique, designers' collection • Linens (bed): Frette.

PART III: Traditional Habits

PACIFIC SYMPHONY
Pages 88-91   Wool moiré (wall upholstery): Clarence House • Rayon/cotton (rope trim): Lee Jofa, Inc. • Leather (bench): J. Robert Scott Textiles, Inc. • Wool (area rug): Sewelson's Carpets International • Wool damask (four George II-style chairs): Manuel Canovas • Wool (carpet): Sewelson's Carpets International • Woven Thai silk (sofa): Robert Scott Textiles, Inc. • Woven Thai silk (wall upholstery): J. Robert Scott Textiles, Inc. • Silk (wall trim): Brunschwig & Fils, Inc. • Wool mohair (lounge chair): Valley Forge Fabrics Inc., trimming from Houlès-U.S.A. • Cotton/linen (slipcovers): Grey Watkins Ltd. • Cotton (flat braided trim, slipcovers): Scalamandré • Douppioni silk (drapery): Randolph & Hein • Cotton sateen (wall upholstery): Roger Arlington Inc. through Kneedler-Fauchère • Cotton moiré (drapery, ottoman, bed drapery, duster and headboard): Clarence House • Silk (trim): Scalamandré •

Wool (Berber-type carpet): Decorative Carpets • Cotton (Battenberg lace bedding): Linens et al • Cotton/rayon velour (lounge chairs): Clarence House • Thai silk (wall upholstery): Jack Lenor Larsen • Silk (wall trim): Brunschwig & Fils, Inc. • Cotton chintz (Roman shade and drapery lining): Zumsteg Ltd. through Kneedler-Fauchère • Cotton chintz (bed drapery): Clarence House • Rayon/cotton (lounge chair): Scalamandré • Rayon (bench in bedroom and ottoman and lounge chairs in sitting area,): Scalamandré • Cotton basket-weave damask (chair): Stroheim & Romann, Inc. • Wool (carpet): Decorative Carpets • Cotton sateen (sofa and lounge chairs, sitting area): Carleton V Ltd.

FRENCH NORMANDY COMFORT
Pages 92-95   Cotton/rayon woven tapestry (dining chairs): Brunschwig & Fils, Inc. • Chenille cotton welting (dining chairs): Brunschwig & Fils, Inc. • Linen/cotton (sheers): Decorators Walk • Glazed cotton print (drapery): "Compagnie des Indes" from Clarence House • Cotton (tablecloth): "Kohat" from Clarence House • Wool (antique Laver-Kirman): Emser International • Cotton, document print (walls): "Savannah Gardens" from Westgate • Wallcovering application: Robert Michaud/Designers Service Studios • Polished cotton (drapery): "Ascot" from Cowtan & Tout through Kneedler-Fauchère • Linen/cotton (sheers) and coverlet: Bassett McNab Co. • Wool (rug): "Clover" from Stark Carpet Corporation • Cotton/silk weave (bench): Robert Crowder & Co. through Keith H. McCoy & Associates • Cotton plaid (wing chair and window seat): Brunschwig & Fils, Inc. • Cotton weave (small armchair): vintage, designers' collection • Polished cotton (drapery): from Cowtan & Tout through Kneedler-Fauchère • Linen/cotton (sheers): Bassett McNab Co.

REINTERPRETING THE PAST
Pages 96-99   Silk/cotton (chairs and drapery): "Cellini Stripe" from Cowtan & Tout • Drapery and trims: fabricated by Jean Pierre André • Cotton velvet (circular seating): "Whittaker" from Ralph Lauren Home Collection • Silk/cotton (drapery): "Cellini Stripe" from Cowtan & Tout • Silk velvet (chair): "Polidoro" from Manuel Canovas • Silk damask (sofa): "Metropolis" from Sahco Hesslein Collection through Bergamo Fabrics Inc. • Wool (antique Tabriz rug): Anthony Foster through Nilo 54 • Drapery and trim: fabricated by Jean Pierre André • Linen/cotton prints (drapery and bed): Mobil Girgi through Manzoni Overseas • Headboard: designed by Pascal Arquitectos, fabricated by Jean Pierre André • Leather (on "Meriggio" chair): Giorgetti S.p.A. through Manzoni Overseas • Cotton-rayon (drapery): "Touret" from Manuel Canovas • Silk (drapery): "Crinkle Damask" from Cowtan & Tout • Silk (sofas): "Defontaine Damask" and "Suffield Stripe" from Cowtan & Tout • Silk (red and gold pillows): "Massena" from André Bon • Silk (celadon chairs): "Chinoiserie Damask" from Cowtan & Tout • Wool (area rug): designed by Pascal Arquitectos, fabricated by Merit • Cotton (drapery and bedspreads): Osborne & Little • Silk print (drapery): through Randolph & Hein, Inc. • Silk stripe (chairs): "Grand Ray" from Mirak Inc. through David Sutherland, Inc. • Wool (area rug): designed by Pascal Arquitectos, fabricated by Merit.

A FEMININE AMBIENCE
Pages 100-103   Printed velvet (sofa and chairs): Lelievre through Carlo Belgir • Cotton (wallcovering): "Empire" from Burger through Carlo Belgir • Silk (covering *tables habillées*): vintage • Aubusson carpet pieces (cushions): vintage • Wool (carpet): Chinese needlepoint through Alberto Levi • Cotton (wallcovering and drapery): Hodsoll McKenzie Silk (bedcovering): vintage • Wool (carpet): Chinese needlepoint through Alberto Levi • Linen (wallcovering and shirred ceiling): Hodsoll McKenzie • Embroidered linen (sheers): through Carlo Belgir • Wool (carpet): English needlepoint through Alberto Levi • Silk taffeta (baldechin): "Du Barry" from Vera Seta through Stoffe D'Arte • Linen (printed floral wallcovering, with handpainted stripes): Bennison Fabrics, Ltd.

TIMELESS CLASSICS
Pages 104-107   Antiqued cotton/rayon velvet (draped on chair): "Chelsea" from Home Couture • Antiqued silk velvet (curtains): "Lorraine" from Home Couture • Silk and silk velvet (drapery): Home Couture • Antiqued cotton velvets (drapery, chairs and throws): Home Couture • Antiqued silk velvets (upholstery): Home Couture • Hand-printed cotton/rayon velvet and hand-printed silk (upholstery): Home Couture • All fabrics (except that on vintage pillows): Home Couture.

A TOUCH OF EUROPE
Pages 108-111   Red cotton toile (living room): "Old Sturbridge Village" by Waverly through F & S Fabrics • Floral rose tapestry (dining room): Diamond Foam & Fabric • Cotton floral with blue ribbon chintz (bedroom): "Alexandra" through Diamond Foam & Fabric • Blue plaid cotton (master bedroom and bed treatment): Diamond Foam & Fabric • Blue country French toile (master bedroom drapery and bed treatment): "Country Living" through Diamond Foam & Fabric • Rayon wool silk (tapestry with a green vine motif): "Fandango" by Caro & Upright/Prudential Fabrics.

GOTHIC FINERY
Pages 112-113   Venetian silk velvet (drapery): "Venezia Velvet" from Lorenzo Rubelli S.p.A. through Bergamo Fabrics Inc.

A CULTIVATED GRACE
Pages 114-115   Bronze silk (drapery and tablecloth): Pindler & Pindler, Inc. • Black cotton stripe (underdrape at table): Pindler & Pindler, Inc. • Silk (braid and tassels): Houlès et Cie. • Faux baby leopard skin leather (chairs): Nancy Corzine • Handpainted-silk light fixture: Noble International through Kneedler-Fauchère • Shirred silk (walls and vanity): Pindler & Pindler, Inc. • Damask linen (chair and ottoman): Pindler & Pindler, Inc. • Handpainted silk (at top and post of four-poster bed): Pindler & Pindler, Inc. • Antique French cotton linen lace (bedcover): collection of Valerie Bernard-Eglit • Sateen cotton (bed skirt and drapery): Pindler & Pindler, Inc. • Cording and tassels (drapery trim): Houlès et Cie. • Cotton voile (sheers): Pindler & Pindler, Inc. • Wool (carpet): Decorative Carpets • Polished cotton (bed hangings, window drapery, duvet cover, top bed skirt and pillows): "Chatham" from Pindler & Pindler, Inc. • Polyester (dust skirt and lining of bed hang-

ings): "Seabreeze" from Pindler & Pindler, Inc. • Silk (French doors): "Princess" from Pindler & Pindler, Inc. • Silk (lounge chair): "Silkkara" from Pindler & Pindler, Inc. • Silk taffeta (ottoman): "Jakarta" from Pindler & Pindler, Inc. • Silk (trims): Houlès et Cie.

RELAXED FORMALITY

Pages 116-117 Silk taffeta (drapery): "Portierre" from Schumacher • Cotton brocade (banquette): Schumacher • Striped cotton striae and leather trim (refectory table): Schumacher • Mohair (sofa): Schumacher • Brushed cotton striae (cigarette table): Schumacher • Silk (pillows on sofa): Schumacher • Silk taffeta and striped moiré (pillows at banquette): Schumacher • Silk/cotton (trim): Schumacher • Cotton damask (dining chairs): Schumacher • Leather, mohair and cotton (stool designed by Sandra Nunnerley): Schumacher • Wool (carpet, border custom-designed by Sandra Nunnerley): Schumacher.

GOSSAMER DREAMS

Pages 118-119 Silk organza (shirred drapery): Barbara Beckmann Designs, Inc. • Layered and handpainted silk (bed treatment and valance): Barbara Beckmann Designs, Inc. • Crushed silk velvet (bench): Barbara Beckmann Designs, Inc. • Cotton moiré (lounge chair): Barbara Beckmann Designs, Inc. • Silk (trimmings): Kenneth Meyer Company • Nylon (carpet): "Hopscotch" from Stark Carpet Corp. • Upholstery fabrication: Knops Upholstery (lounge chair), Fabrications for Interiors (all other).

SEDUCTIVE SOPHISTICATION

Pages 120-123 Cotton (bedspread): Randolph & Hein, Inc. • Linen (bed drapery): Randolph & Hein, Inc. • Cotton (pillow with blue flange): Meridian Linens • Cotton denim (portieres and balloon drapery): Henry Calvin Fabrics • Silk (lining, portiere and balloon drapery): Randolph & Hein, Inc. • Silk (striped drapery): Randolph & Hein, Inc. • Cotton (sheers): Randolph & Hein, Inc. • Cotton (chair slipcover): Lee Jofa, Inc. • Cotton terrycloth and lace (towels): Frette S.p.A. • Horsehair (black cushion): designer's collection • Cashmere (throw): Meridian Linens • Wool (antique Aubusson carpet): Y & B Boulour Carpets • Drapery/upholstery fabrication: Susan Lind Chastain Sewing.

PART IV: Natural Imprints

DIALOGUE WITH NATURE

Pages 126-127 Cotton duck (upholstered furniture): Flexform S.p.A. • Linen/cotton (drapery): Etamine SA • Wool (Oriental rug, nineteenth-century): Galleria Hermitage • Cotton (settee and skylight closure): Bennison Fabrics, Ltd. • Wool (area rug): "Rohan" by Nanda Vigo for Follies Collection from Driade S.p.A. • Wool (carpet): from Sit-in Pietro Radici Tappettifico Nazionale S.p.A.

WEEKEND HABIT

Pages 128-131 Linen (slipcovers): Donghia Furniture/Textiles • Linen cotton damask (pillows): "Fat Stripe" from Donghia Furniture/Textiles • Handwoven cotton (striped sofa): "Hamaca Rojo" from Donghia Furniture/Textiles.

RANCHO DIABLO

Pages 132-133 Woven-cotton flamestitch (sofa): Schumacher.

WINE COUNTRY NATIVE

Pages 134-135 Silk taffeta (drapery): "Celadon and Pearl Stripe" • Handpainted silk (wall hanging): "Midnight Garden" • Silk (jacket): "Winter Stripe" • Silk (lounge chair): "Silk Leaves" • Silk taffeta (drapery): "Celadon Stripe" with "Pearl" border • Blue-and-white cotton print (pillows and lounge): "Ginza Fish" • Red cotton print (pillow): "Ginza Babies" • Silk taffeta: "Jade Topaz Stripe" • Silk/linen: "Amber Floral" and "Plaintains."

BAREFOOT AND HAPPY

Pages 136-137 Linen cottons: Ralph Lauren Home Collection, Clarence House, Le Décor Française • Floral cotton print (ceiling): Laura Ashley • Floral cotton print (walls): Ralph Lauren Home Collection • Cotton (area rugs): Malmaison Antiques • Sea grass (floorcovering): Malmaison Antiques.

CAPE COD LIGHTLY

Pages 138-139 Rayon/cotton linen (sofa): Manuel Canovas • Woven-cotton rayon (wing chair at fireplace): Scalamandré • Wool (rug): Sally Vowell, weaver/Allegro Rug Weavers • Cotton (four chairs at round table): Gretchen Bellinger Inc. • Leather (ottoman): Spinneybeck • Wool Lurex (drapery): Gretchen Bellinger • Woven-linen chenille (chairs and ottomans): Donghia Furniture/Textiles • Woven-linen cotton chenille (throw): Jeffrey Arnoff, Inc. • Cotton (rug), custom-colored: Thomas K. Woodard American Antiques & Quilts • Woven raffia (headboard): J. Robert Scott Textiles, Inc. • Egyptian cotton (boudoir and neckroll pillows): "Swirls" from Trousseau through Feather Your Nest • Viscose/rayon (bench and window seat cushions): Lee Jofa • Cotton viscose (window seat cushion): Brunschwig & Fils, Inc. • Needlepoint (pillows): custom through Sprott-Nichols Design.

BEACHFRONT SERENITY

Pages 140-141 Polyester (sheers): Henry Calvin Fabrics • Leather (beige armchair and ottoman): Dakota Jackson, Inc. • Cotton velvet (blue armchair and ottoman): The Knoll Group • Wool (carpet): custom design, fabricated by Patterson, Flynn, Martin & Manges, Inc. • Silk (curtains): Jack Lenor Larsen • Wool/rayon (sofa): Clarence House • Silk/cotton (cushions on stools by window): Donghia Furniture/Textiles.

REINCARNATIONS

Pages 142-143 Silk: Fortuny • Haitian cotton (drapery): Waverly • Cotton (drapery trim): M&J Trimmings • Wool (carpet and trim): Einstein Moomjy.

A DELICATE PEACE

Pages 144-147 Framing fabrics - Cotton chenille, laminated to frame: Pollack & Associates; Douppioni silk, laminated to mat: Barbara Beckmann Designs, Inc.; Thai silk, fillet: Jim Thompson Thai Silk • Fabrics on worktable: Old World Weavers; J.Robert Scott Textiles, Inc.; Rodolph Inc.; Sahco-Hesslein Collection through Bergamo Fabrics Inc.; Henry Calvin; Schumacher; Jim Thompson Thai Silks; Leslie Hannon Custom Trims • Cotton/wool/nylon chenille (drafting chair):

Pollack & Associates • Vest (back of chair) - Cotton chenille tapestry (face): Glant Textiles Corporation; Thai silk (lining): Jim Thompson Thai Silk • Heywood Wakefield rocker - Thai silk (upholstery): Jim Thompson Thai Silks; Rayon (upholstery trim): Mark Hampton Signature Collection through Kravet; Acrylic chenille throw: David S. Gibson Custom Weavers • Fish pillow on rocker - Handscreened douppioni silk: Barbara Beckmann Designs, Inc.; Metallic cord: Bargia Trims through Clifford-Stephens, Inc. • Striped pillow on rocker - Cotton blend: Old World Weavers; Cotton/Rayon rope: Schumacher • Loft - Cotton chenille (contoured bedcover and flat flange): Pollack & Associates; Wool-blend tapestry (face of throw): S. Harris & Co.; Cotton chenille tapestry (throw lining): Glant Textiles Corporation • Loft pillows, (clockwise) from left - Wool-blend tapestry: S. Harris & Co., with cotton multi-fringe from Westgate; Rayon-blend woven tapestry: Schumacher, with metallic cord from Bargia Trims; Cotton chenille tapestry: Glant Textiles Corporation, with curly fringe from Mark Hampton Signature Collection • Door scarf treatment - Douppioni silk (scarf and panel lining): Barbara Beckmann Designs, Inc.; Hand-screened douppioni silk (panel face): Barbara Beckmann Designs, Inc.; Metallic cord: Bargia Trims through Clifford-Stephens, Inc. • Copy machine cover - Silk (body): Henry Calvin Fabrics; Thai silk (flange): Jim Thompson Thai Silks; Hand-screened silk appliqué: Barbara Beckmann Designs, Inc. • Flower pouche - Douppioni silk (pouch): Barbara Beckmann Designs, Inc.; Hand-screened douppioni silk appliqué: Barbara Beckmann Designs, Inc.; Metallic cord: Bargia Trims through Clifford-Stephens, Inc. • Flower pot bag (on plant stand) - Thai silk (bag): Jim Thompson Thai Silk; Metallic cord: Bargia Trims through Clifford-Stephens, Inc. • Textiles fabrications: C.J.'s Custom Draperies • Upholstery: Lanzetti Custom Upholstering.

SPINNING YARNS

Pages 148-149 Handpainted fabrics (drapery, side chairs, lounge chair & ottoman): custom designed and created for Clodagh by The Ashley Studio. Base Fabrics incorporating Hoechst Celanese fibers were selected from various sources. • Wool (area rugs): Clodagh for Palazzetti, Inc. • Viscose/cotton (sofa): "Caracul" from Pollack & Associates • Rayon chenille (throw): Jeffrey Aronoff, Inc. • Polyester (drapery and fabric sculpture, hallway ceiling): ESP extra strength performance fiber from Hoechst Celanese in a woven fabric from Fairlane Incorporated • Silk (pillows): Indian import through Etiket • Pillow fabrication: Etiket • Woven bamboo (shades): Conrad Imports, Inc. through Jack Lenor Larsen • Douppioni silk (pillows): Carolyn Quartermaine through Agnes Bourne, Inc. • Silk canvas (large seat cushions): Jack Lenor Larsen, printed with a French script designed by Carolyn Quartermaine.

GETAWAY MODES

Pages 150-151 Spandex (fabric sculpture): Lycra from Elastic Fabric of America • Polyester (fabric structure): ESP Extra Stretch Performance yarn from Hoechst Celanese, fabric from Fairlane Incorporated.

DIRECTORY

Linda Abernathy
159 South Rodeo Drive
Beverly Hills, California 90212
United States
Tel: (310) 271-8558
Fax: (310) 271-0441

Ace Architects
David Weingarten
Lucia Howard
330 Second Street
Oakland, California 94607
United States
Tel: (510) 452-0775
Fax: (510) 452-1175

Reginald Adams, IIDA
Reginald Adams & Associates
8500 Melrose Avenue, Suite 207
Los Angeles, California 90069
United States
Tel: (310) 659-8038
Fax: (310) 659-8594

Giancarlo Alhadeff, AIA
Studio Giancarlo Alhadeff
Viale Majno, 5
20122 Milan
Italy
Tel: (39) 2 76 00 87 22
Fax: (39) 2 76 00 95 60

Edward Carson Beall
Edward Carson Beall
& Associates
23727 Hawthorne Boulevard
Torrance, California 90505
United States
Tel: (310) 378-1280
Fax: (310) 375-9530

Barbara Beckmann
Barbara Beckmann
Designs, Inc.
2425 17th Street
San Francisco, California 94110
United States
Tel: (415) 863-0304
Fax: (415) 863-6679

Bedell-Laughlin & Associates
Marjorie A. Bedell, FASID
Lawrence G. Laughlin
6061 West Third Street
Los Angeles, California 90036
United States
Tel: (213) 930-2802
Fax: (213) 935-5132

Lisbeth Beise, IIDA
Indigo
P.O. Box 1005
Wilson, Wyoming 83014
United States
Tel: (307) 739-9723
also, in Hong Kong:
Tel: (852) 2849 7714
Fax: (852) 2849 4087

Sig Bergamin
Sig Bergamin Interiors, Inc.
20 East 69th Street, #3C
New York, New York 10021
United States
Tel: (212) 861-4515
Fax: (212) 861-3667

Valerie Bernard-Eglit
6113 Oakbridge Drive
Granite Bay, California 95746
United States
Tel: (916) 791-2839
Fax: (916) 791-4960

Joseph Braswell, ASID
Joseph Braswell & Associates
425 East 58th Street
New York, New York 10022
United States
Tel: (212) 688-1075
Fax: (212) 752-7167

Marcie Vesel Bronkar
Home Couture
893 South Lucerne Boulevard
Los Angeles, California 90005
United States
Tel: (213) 936-1302
Fax: (213) 936-8265

Erika Brunson
Erika Brunson Design
Associates
903 Westbourne Drive
Los Angeles, California 90069
United States
Tel: (310) 652-1970
Fax: (310) 652-2381

Arthur de Mattos Casas
Casas E Ediçoes de Design
Al. Casa Branca, 1136
CEP 01408
São Paulo
Brazil
Tel: (55) 11 282 6311
Fax: (55) 11 282 6608

Joel and Margaret Chen
J.F. Chen Antiques
8414 Melrose Avenue
Los Angeles, California 90069
United States
Tel: (213) 655-6310
Fax: (213) 655-9689

Clodagh Design International
Clodagh
Robert Pierpont
365 First Avenue
New York, New York 10010
United States
Tel: (212) 673-9202
Fax: (212) 614-9125

Lorraine Crockford
Lorraine Crockford Design
24065 Ocean Avenue
Torrance, California 90505
United States
Tel: (310) 373-8685

Sherri Donghia
Donghia
485 Broadway
New York, New York 10013
United States
Tel: (212) 925-2777
Fax: (212) 925-4819

John David Edison
John David Edison Interior
Design Inc.
2 Berkeley Street, Suite 301
Toronto, Ontario
Canada M5A 2W3
Tel: (416) 359-1717
Fax: (416) 359-1715

Rand Elliott, FAIA
Elliott + Associates Architects
35 Harrison Avenue
Oklahoma City, Oklahoma 73104
United States
Tel: (405) 232-9554
Fax: (405) 232-9997

Mark Enos
Enos & Co.
705 North Alfred Street
Los Angeles, California 90069
United States
Tel: (213) 655-0109
Fax: (213) 655-7719

Roger Eulau
300 East 34th Street
New York, New York 10016
United States
Tel: (212) 686-5687
Fax: (212) 889-6191

Everage Interior Design
John C. Everage
Krista Everage, ASID
1025 24th Street
Santa Monica, California 90403
United States
Tel: (310) 264-0066
Fax: (310) 264-0091

Susan Federman, CCIDC
Susan Federman Interior
Design
250 Laurel Street, Suite 301
San Francisco, California 94118
United States
Tel: (415) 563-1184
Fax: (415) 776-5617

Karen Foote
24432 Southwest Gage Road
Wilsonville, Oregon 97070
United States

Victoria Hagan
Victoria Hagan Interiors
654 Madison Avenue, Penthouse 2201
New York, New York 10021
United States
Tel: (212) 888-1178
Fax: (212) 888-0974

Meryl Hare, MSIDA, MDIA
Hare & Klein Pty Ltd.
11 Chuter Street
McMahoons Point
New South Wales 2060
Australia
Tel: (61) 2 954 0780
Fax: (61) 2 955 4896

Allison A. Holland, ASID
Creative Decorating
168 Poloke Place
Honolulu, Hawaii 96822
United States
Tel: (808) 955-1465
Fax: (808) 949-2290

Charles Jacobsen, Inc.
Charles Jacobsen
Brad Blair
Pacific Design Center, Space G679
8687 Melrose Avenue
Los Angeles, California 90069
United States
Tel: (310) 652-1188
Fax: (310) 652-2555

Ronn Jaffe, Inc.
Mars Jaffe, ASID
Ronn Jaffe, ASID, IIDA
The Design Studio Building
9204 Harrington Drive
Potomac, Maryland 20854
United States
Tel: (301) 365-3500
Fax: (301) 365-3157

Jack Lenor Larsen
Larsen Design Studio
41 East 11th Street
New York, New York 10003-4685
United States
Tel: (212) 674-3993
Fax: (212) 674-1426

Richard Lear
Richard Lear Design
30 Main Street
Southampton, New York 11968
United States
Tel: (516) 283-0272
Fax: (516) 287-4498

Daniela Leusch
Via Gian Giacomo Moro 12
20123 Milan
Italy
Tel/Fax: (39) 2 58 10 28 76

Emanuela Frattini
Magnusson, Architect
588 Broadway
New York, New York 10012
United States
Tel: (212) 925-4500
Fax: (212) 925-4525

Richard Mayhew
Mayhew Design
705 N. Alfred Street
Los Angeles, California 90069
United States
Tel: (213) 655-0737
Fax: (213) 655-7719

Joszi Meskan, ASID
Joszi Meskan Associates
479 Ninth Street
San Francisco, California 94103
United States
Tel: (415) 431-0500
Fax: (415) 431-9339

Mike Moore
Mike Moore Studio
2100 Jackson Street
San Francisco, California 94115
United States
Tel: (415) 567-7955
Fax: (415) 567-7986

Joan Moseley, ASID, CCID
Joan Moseley Design
649 La Loma Road
Pasadena, California 91105
United States
Tel: (818) 799-1578
Fax: (818) 799-6967

James Northcutt Associates
James Northcutt
Darrell Schmitt, ASID, CID
717 North La Cienega Boulevard
Los Angeles, California 90069
United States
Tel: (310) 659-8595
Fax: (310) 659-7120

Sandra Nunnerley
Sandra Nunnerley, Inc.
112 East 71st Street
New York, New York 10022
United States
Tel: (212) 472-9341
Fax: (212) 472-9346

Olson/Sundberg
Architects, Inc.
James Olson
Tom Kundig
108 First Avenue South, 4th floor
Seattle, Washington 98104
United States
Tel: (206) 624-5670
Fax: (206) 624-3730

Pascal Arquitectos
S.A. de C.V.
Carlos Pascal
Gerard Pascal
Atlaltunco #99
Tecamachalco Edo de Mexico
C.P. 53950 Mexico
Tel: (525) 294 2371
Fax: (525) 294 8513

Piero Pinto
Piero Pinto, S.R.L.
Viale Majno, 5
Milan
Italy
Tel: (39) 2 78 27 03
Fax: (39) 2 76 02 25 66

Powell/Kleinschmidt
Donald D. Powell
Robert D. Kleinschmidt
645 North Michigan Avenue, Suite 810
Chicago, Illinois 60611
United States
Tel: (312) 642-6450
Fax: (312) 642-5135

Geoffrey Scott
GSDA
2917 1/2 Main Street
Santa Monica, California 90294
United States
Tel: (310) 396-5416
Fax: (310) 399-5246

Oscar Shamamian, AIA
Fergusson Murray &
Shamamian, Architects
270 LaFayette Street
New York, New York 10012
United States
Tel: (212) 941-8088
Fax: (212) 941-8089

Marjorie Shushan
Marjorie Shushan, Inc.
15 West 53rd Street
New York, New York 10019
United States
Tel: (212) 975-1200
Fax: (212) 975-0097

Mary Siebert
Siebert & Associates
1415 Second Avenue South
Seattle, Washington 98101
United States
Tel/Fax: (206) 621-7676

Sprott-Nichols Design
Gari Sprott, ASID
John Nichols
335 Madison
San Antonio, Texas 78204
United States
Tel: (210) 224-1885
Fax: (210) 224-1887

Gisela Stromeyer
Gisela Stromeyer
Architectural Design
57 Jay Street
Brooklyn, New York 11201
United States
Tel: (718) 797-1803
Fax: (718) 858-0024

Mary Tait
Mary Tait Co.
2501 Constance Street
New Orleans, Louisiana 70130
United States
Tel: (504) 899-1048

Stan Taylor
E.N.T. incorporated
8479 Steller Drive
Culver City, California 90232
United States
Tel: (310) 202-6162
Fax: (310) 202-6706

Christine Van der Hurd
305 Riverside Drive
New York, New York 10025
United States
Tel: (212) 666-1234
Fax: (212) 666-1245

Marianne van Lent
430 Greenwich Street
New York, New York 10013
United States
Tel: (212) 431-4249

Annie Walwyn-Jones Ltd.
305 Riverside Drive
New York, New York 10025
United States
Tel: (212) 666-1234
Fax: (212) 666-1245

Carla Weisberg
47 West 12th Street
New York, New York 10011
United States
Tel/Fax: (212) 627-7632

Mark Zeff
Mark Zeff Consulting Group
260 West 72nd Street, Suite 12B
New York, New York 10023
United States
Tel: (212) 580-7090
Fax: (212) 580-7181

Robert G. Zinkhan Jr., AIA
1632 Deer Run
Santa Rosa, California 95405
United States
Tel: (707) 579-2170

Isao Aihara
3-5-22-201 Kamitakaido
Suginami-ku Tokyo 168
Japan
Tel: 03-3290-4787
Fax: 03-5496-9508

Michael Arden
14568 Greenleaf Street
Sherman Oaks, California 91403
United States
Tel: (310) 274-2064

Jaime Ardiles-Arce
730 Fifth Avenue
New York, New York 10019
United States
Tel: (212) 333-8779
Fax: (212) 593-2070

Daniel Aubry
Daniel Aubry Studio
365 First Avenue
New York, New York 10010
United States
Tel: (212) 598-4190
Fax: (212) 505-7670

Victor Benitez
Guanajuato 130
Co. Roma
Mexico, D.F. CP 06700
Tel: (525) 574-8032

Robert Emmett Bright
Localita La Svolta, 54
05018 Orvieto (Terni)
Italy
Tel: 07 6392948

Steven Brooke
7910 SW 54th Court
Miami, Florida 33142
United States
Tel: (305) 667-8075
Fax: (305) 663-0405

Billy Cunningham
26 St. Mark's Place
New York, New York 10003
United States
Tel: (212) 677-4904

Alessandro De Crignis
Localita La Svolta, 54
05018 Orvieto (Terni)
Italy
Tel: 07 6392948

Feliciano
29 W. 38th Street
New York, New York 10018
Tel: (212) 354-7683

Scott Frances/ESTO
31 Harrison Street
New York, New York 10013
United States
Tel/Fax: (212) 529-6642

PHOTOGRAPHERS

Tina Freeman
The Decatur Studio
1040 Magazine Street
New Orleans, Louisiana 70130
United States
Tel: (504) 523-3000
Fax: (504) 581-4397

David Glomb
458 1/2 N. Genesee Avenue
Los Angeles, California 90036
United States
Tel: (213) 655-4491
Fax: (213) 651-1437

Rob Gray
160 West End Avenue
New York, New York 10023
United States
Tel: (212) 721-3240
Fax: (212) 721-1192

John Hall
885 Tenth Avenue
New York, New York 10019
United States
Tel: (212) 757-0369

Hedrich-Blessing
11 West Illinois Street
Chicago, Illinois 60610
United States
Tel: (312) 321-1151
Fax: (312) 321-1165

Michael Jensen
655 NW 76th
Seattle, Washington 98117
United States
Tel: (206) 778-7963

Elliott Kaufman
Elliott Kaufman Photography
255 West 90th Street
New York, New York 10024
United States
Tel: (212) 496-0860

David Livingston
1036 Erica Road
Mill Valley, California 94941
United States
Tel: (415) 383-0898
Fax: (415) 383-0897

Nola Lopez
200 Varick Street, #508
New York, New York 10014
United States
Tel: (212) 645-4348
Fax: (212) 645-8826

Thomas Mayfried
Zentner Strasse 18
D-80798 Munich
Germany
Tel: (89) - 2725861
Fax: (89) - 2725863

Norman McGrath
164 West 79th Street
New York, New York 10024
United States
Tel: (212) 799-6422
Fax: (212) 799-1285

Jon Miller
Hedrich-Blessing
11 West Illinois Street
Chicago, Illinois 60610
United States
Tel: (312) 321-1151
Fax: (312) 321-1165

Do Do Jin Ming
Do Do Jin
Lower G.F. No. 1
5F Bowen Road - The Peak
Hong Kong
Tel/Fax: (852) 2522-5084

Michael Moran
245 Mulberry #14
New York, New York 10012
United States
Tel: (212) 226-2596
Fax: (212) 219-1566

Michael Mundy
220 East 5th Street
New York, New York 10003
United States
Tel: (212) 529-7114
Fax: (212) 753-4804

Mary Nichols
Mary E. Nichols Photography
132 So. Beechwood Drive
Los Angeles, California 90004
United States
Tel: (213) 935-3080
Fax: (213) 935-9788

Anthony Peres
Anthony Peres Photography
645 Oxford Avenue
Venice, California 90291
United States
Tel/Fax: (301) 821-1984

Tuca Reinés
Rua Emanuel Kant, 58
São Paulo
Brazil
Tel: 011-8519127
Fax: 011-8528735

Hugo Rojas
Hugo Rojas Photography
2020 N. Main Street, #231
Los Angeles, California 90031
United States
Tel/Fax: (213) 222-8836

Douglas Sandberg
Douglas Sandberg
Photography
158 South Park
San Francisco, California 94107
United States
Tel: (415) 882-9871
Fax: (415) 882-9552

Bob Shimer
Hedrich-Blessing
11 West Illinois Street
Chicago, Illinois 60610
United States
Tel: (312) 321-1151
Fax: (312) 321-1165

Studio Acqua Snc.
Riccardo Gusmaroli
Domenico Iacopino
Via Vignola 15
Milano
Italy
Tel: 02 5455805

David Valenzuela
1843 S. Arapahoe
Los Angeles, California 90006
United States
Tel: (213) 748-0644
Fax: (213) 748-7976

John Vaughan
John Vaughan & Associates
17315 Via Frances
San Lorenzo, California 94580
United States
Tel: (510) 481-9814

Peter Vitale
Peter Vitale Photography
P.O. Box 10126
Santa Fe, New Mexico 87504
United States
Tel: (505) 988-2558
Fax: (505) 982-6412

Dominique Vorillon
1636 Silverwood Terrace
Los Angeles, California 90026
United States
Tel: (213) 660-5883

Richard Waugh
9A Alpha Road
Willoughby 2068
New South Wales
Tel/Fax: 02 9587425

Mark Wieland
3836 Fulton St., N.W.
Washington, D.C. 20007
United States
Tel: (202) 333-5295

Alan Weintraub
2325 Third Street, Suite 325A
San Francisco, California 94107
United States
Tel: (415) 553-8191
Fax: (415) 553-8192

INDEX

ACKNOWLEDGMENTS

Having benefited twice before from its high standards in the publication of *Empowered Spaces* (now released as *At Home & At Work*) and *Furniture: Architects' & Designers' Originals*, I am thrilled to have the opportunity to write four more books for PBC International, Inc. These four volumes were conceived as a series on the residential use of tile, stone & brick; wood; glass; and fabric. Their development could not have been possible without the extraordinary commitment of Publisher Mark Serchuck and Managing Director Penny Sibal to good design. That Managing Editor Susan Kapsis has overseen and scrutinized their development fills me with a sense of security. Besides, with our interests being similar and our enthusiasm high, we have had a marvelous time!

PBC's Technical Director Richard Liu has again lent his expert analysis to make sure that only excellent photographic material prevails. And Garrett Schuh's design, sensitive to the subject, has kept me in a constant state of excitement. The art department's Barbara Ann Cast proved indispensable to the final execution of the layout. And to the editorial department for perfecting every detail—a million bouquets! I was also most fortunate to have had the admirably thorough Angeline Vogl proofread every word.

I am grateful to the many architects, designers and photographers whose work fills the pages of this book, as well as to the homeowners who have so generously shared their living spaces for publication. And finally, I am indebted to Stanley Abercrombie for graciously contributing the foreword which appears in each of the four books in the series.